Loving Me

CLAUDETTE SIMS

Loving Me

A Sisterfriend's Guide to Being Single and Happy

An Owl Book

HENRY HOLT AND COMPANY   NEW YORK

Henry Holt and Company, Inc.
Publishers since 1866
115 West 18th Street
New York, New York 10011

Henry Holt® is a registered
trademark of Henry Holt and Company, Inc.

Library of Congress Cataloging-in-Publication Data
Sims, Claudette E. (Claudette Elaine)
Loving me : a sisterfriend's guide to being single and happy / Claudette
Sims.—1st ed.
p.   cm.
"An owl book."
ISBN 0-8050-5160-0 (pbk.)
1. Single women—United States—Psychology.   2. Afro-American single
people—Psychology.   3. Self-esteem in women.   I. Title.
HQ800.4.U6S535   1999
646.7'0086'52—dc21   98-24341

First Edition 1999

Designed by Kate Nichols

Printed in the United States of America
All first editions are printed on acid-free paper. ∞

10   9   8   7   6   5   4   3   2   1

To my aunt Gladys,

who departed this life on December 26, 1978,

and to my mother, Evangeline,

who is a living, breathing example of

the strength, courage, and endurance

of women everywhere

Contents

Loving Me

1

Loving Yourself

"The busy have no time for tears."

eing single is not an illness or a disease. It is not contagious or inflammatory. It is not a condition. It is a state of being. *Single* simply means not married or currently involved in a meaningful relationship, period. Being single sometimes means being alone but it doesn't necessarily mean being lonely. In fact, there is seldom a good excuse for being lonely. As reasonably attractive, reasonably intelligent, and reasonably successful single women, we can't afford to spend a good portion of our lives waiting for someone else out there in never-never land to fulfill our dreams, make us happy, and help us feel complete.

Loving Me is a book for women who understand that each of us has been given a unique opportunity to create our own joy, our own moments and memories. It is a book for women who are not just marking time, waiting to exhale, but rather have decided to go for the gusto now . . . today . . . the only time that is promised to us. This is not a rehearsal for life. We only go around once and this is it. But once is all you need if you take responsibility for your life and squeeze every drop of love, joy, and happiness from every moment of every day.

As little girls growing up, very few of us ever seriously thought that we would have to go through life alone, without a mate. We imagined that there would be someone to love us, to take care of us, to help make our life complete. As adults, though, we have come to face some alarming realities: There are an estimated 47 million single women in the United States and only 41 million single men. In the African American community, the numbers are also discouraging: According to the U.S. Census Bureau (March 1996), there are 8.3 million single Black women to 6.4 million single Black men. Subtract the teenagers (unless you want to go to jail), the undesirables, and the number of unavailable men, and the pool of eligible Black men becomes even smaller.

In this book, we're going to talk about single women deserving and achieving happiness and maintaining a positive outlook on relationships even when they're not in one. We want to encourage women who may be emotionally paralyzed from the excess baggage they have been carrying around as a result of past mistakes they may have made with men. It is no secret that the Black family is in trouble, so *Loving Me* is also an attempt to address some of the rocky issues that prevent men and women from understanding one another as well as their need to build solid relationships.

There are several major obstacles that often stand in the way as we try to connect.

1. Our biggest problem is that we don't trust each other. Trust is the foundation of any lasting relationship. Without trust, true love rarely has a chance to flourish and grow. It's almost impossible to commit your heart and body and soul to someone

that you don't trust and can't depend on. And it doesn't make a lot of sense to put your confidence in men who betray your trust, who lie and cheat and steal their way into lonely hearts and then leave their footprints there.

2. Another serious concern is communication. Relationships are often defined by how well the parties communicate. Communicating effectively and honestly is what connects people. A good connection allows people to express their feelings and to ask for what they want and need without fear of being misunderstood or ridiculed. No communication . . . no connection.

3. Sharing similar value systems is a must. The goals we set, both personally and professionally, are influenced by what we think is important. It's crucial that the partners we choose care about the same things we do.

Women are especially vulnerable to the pain and disappointment of romantic relationships. I believe this is primarily because we choose to love Black men no matter what. While many Black women are pursuing the American dream in record numbers, record numbers of Black men are pursuing alcohol and drugs and guns. Because corporate America is less intimidated by Black women, there are more Black women employed. But Black men have to take some of the responsibility for being unemployable and for getting more excited about making a living through illegal means than legal ones. We can't cop out by blaming racism for everything, true or not. We have to take our individual destiny into our own hands by taking education more seriously and planning for a career that will enhance our self-esteem. We must take care of ourselves first in order to take care of our lover, our family, and ultimately our community.

We know that there are definitely some together brothers out there, but let's face it, there seems to be a greater number of together sisters. Many sisters feel they have no choice, so even though they're smart, attractive, and successful, they are settling for no-win situations with men who are available but not necessarily compatible intellectually and socially. Settling for anybody with a pulse just to avoid spending a Friday night alone is not the answer.

Loving Me is a survival guide for single women who have had enough—enough lies, games, and pain. It's for women who have been looking in all the wrong places and choosing all the wrong men. It's also for single women—twenty-five or thirty-five or fifty-five—who have finally decided they alone are responsible for their happiness.

Sure, some women may choose to sit at home and crochet Christmas gifts in April, clean out the refrigerator every Friday night, or sing the I'm-not-married-yet blues and cry themselves to sleep every other night. It's definitely easier to play the role of victim, but just because you're single doesn't mean you're powerless. Just imagine: As a single person, you can do something every day that makes you happy or improves the quality of your life without having to worry about what *he* has done *now*.

Look in the mirror and say hello to the person who is going to enable you to live the kind of life you deserve. We have to spend as much time or more in choosing a man as we do in choosing our clothes and makeup. Often, we blindly step over the few good men (and there are some) to get to the bastards who abuse us over and over. We keep begging the wrong people to stay—and then wonder why we keep getting dumped on.

Take control of your life: If you don't like going out with someone with whom you have absolutely nothing in common but who is always available, stop doing it. If you don't like sleeping with someone who doesn't satisfy your needs or waking up with someone you wish would hurry up and leave, stop doing it.

In other words, if you don't like your life, change it! Take charge of yourself and your life. Make room in your world for some quiet time. Get to know who you really are—think about what makes you happy. Then do some of those things. Treat yourself to a manicure or even a cruise. When you're happy and satisfied with your life, you'll have so much more to give to the people who need you and love you—and that includes yourself.

You have to work at being happy, just as people unconsciously work at being unhappy. Learn how to chase away the blues before they become too deeply rooted in your soul. When I feel a bout of depression coming on, I usually listen to inspirational music or call a friend who is always positive and affirming. Or I take a long, leisurely bath, get lost in a good book, or treat myself to dinner at a fine restaurant. I try to dispose of any negative beliefs that stand in the way of my getting on with my life at that moment—for example, I'm too fat, all the good men are taken, I'm going to be single for the rest of my life. Whenever we're tempted to give into feelings of self-pity or self-defeat, we should stand in the mirror and practice telling loneliness, depression, anxiety, and fear to go to hell!

To achieve happiness, you have to be able to see it and feel it. Happiness should ooze out of us in our bright smiles and hopeful attitudes. But you can't find happiness if your eyes are always clouded with tears and your heart is overflowing with self-pity. Make a promise today to stop feeling sorry for yourself because you can't find Mr. Right. Let's look for something else in life worth loving and living for, especially ourselves. With all our flaws and imperfections, hurts and fears, we're still worth loving.

Loving Me is about loving—loving from the inside out. Love starts in our hearts and moves out into the other hearts of the world. We must stop saving up all our love for the Maybe Man and start spending some of that love on ourselves, filling our own hearts and souls with joy and happiness and peace. We must learn to fall in love with ourselves, so if we never meet that special person with whom we thought we'd spend the rest of our lives, we will still feel loved.

It is my wish that this book will show you how important it is to believe that one is a perfect number. You don't have to spend your life waiting for someone to make you feel pretty or special or loved. You can do that for yourself; you can learn to love, nurture, and pamper yourself.

I hope this book will convince you that you do not have to live a marginal life just because you're single. That you will come to realize that you are not helpless and your life is not hopeless. That you can create the kind of life that you want by learning to embrace yourself and your dreams, by having the courage to take charge of your life.

2

The Great American Illusion

"Wisdom is immortal."

For centuries, marriage has been regarded as an American tradition. However, the ugly statistics of the '80s and '90s reveal that many men and women have made the difficult decision to end twenty- or thirty-year marriages in search of happiness. Today, more than one million marriages end in divorce each year. The dissolution of so many marriages serves to remind us that in the life process—from birth to death—marriage is simply a stage. Sometimes short, sometimes long, but a stage nevertheless, such as grade school, puberty, or a new job.

Women need to be deprogrammed on the subject of marriage. We must learn to see marriage as a pleasant, but not necessary, stage in our growth. So many of us cling to the one-day-when-I-am-married fantasy that keeps us from living in the present. It's time to challenge the system that has historically forced us into "singles court."

The charge? "You mean you're twenty-five (or thirty or forty) and not married yet? What's wrong with you, girl? What are you waiting for? You're not getting any younger! You must be too picky! What's the deal?" The deal is that it's none of their business. And we must learn to tell them that, firmly, in the spirit of love and with a smile on our face. Such newfound attitudes and responses will undoubtedly have a chilling effect on the "singles police," and we'll be better off because of it.

Yet we must also do some self-examination and question our own fears about living our lives without that special someone that we can proudly refer to as our "hussssband" four or five times an hour. We must learn to celebrate the choices that being single offers us. One of the major accomplishments of the civil rights movement—in addition to riding at the front of the bus, and eating in downtown restaurants—was our right to choose.

With this gift of choice, however, come major responsibilities. We can choose to become a slave to thoughts and feelings that make us feel inferior because we are alone. Or we can take charge of our lives and tell our feelings (which are always temporal) to go to hell! We can allow ourselves to be enslaved by daydreams of love and marriage twenty-four hours a day or allow love to become a slave to *us* by making this journey called life a blast!

We can make a decision to take responsibility for our own hurts or get hurt over and over. We can react to every negative comment about why we can't find Mr. Right ("you want too much, you're too proud/mean/thin/fat/short/tall," whatever). Or we can detach ourselves from these detractors, love them from a distance, and get on with our lives. The point is that we get to choose. Good or bad. Right or wrong. We get to choose!

How did we fall into this trap in the first place? Who said that everybody had to be married? What gives society the right to define who I am by whether I have a little gold band on the third finger of my left hand? Who gives people permission to ask me (and all of my unmarried friends) over and over, "Why aren't you married?" Besides being rude, it's not anyone's business.

The truth is that society did not prepare some of us for the roles we're being forced to play today. We grew up as many little girls—Black *and* White—did in the '50s and '60s: reading about Cinderella (I still can't believe she was hooked on a guy with a shoe fetish). We met Snow White and the Seven Dwarfs (hardly a virgin after shacking up with seven little horny dudes in Jane Fonda tights). We watched *Father Knows Best, Leave It to Beaver,* and *The Donna Reed Show* and began to shape and mold our future based on these superficial television families. It was not until after I was grown up that I found out that not even White families lived these fairy-tale existences. It's not that we were naive or stupid. We knew that television was supposed to be make-believe, but these make-believe families gave us a pattern for a perfect life.

Not only have these distortions been detrimental to Black women (because, frankly, we watch more television) but the distortions have been detrimental to every woman who was led to believe that all little girls grow up, learn to cook and sew, marry the boy next door, move into the white house with the picket fence (or the two-story condo with the attached garage), become housewives and mothers, deliver a boy and a girl (in that order), and are happy for the rest of their life.

It's easy to criticize television, the system, and everybody else for the deceptions and distortions that many of us grew up claiming as our reality. But the truth of the matter is that in a fervent attempt to give their children better lives and help them tolerate (not accept) their second-class citizenship in America, a lot of Black parents neglected to help their children differentiate between what was possible and what was probable.

Please don't misunderstand. I'm not saying that finding a suitable mate, getting married, and living a comfortable, middle-class existence is beyond the grasp of all young Black couples. It most certainly isn't. Young Black men and women are getting married every day and the Black middle-class has experienced dynamic growth in the last twenty-five years. Nationwide, colleges and universities are turning out thousands of bright, educated, ambitious African American students—though, admittedly, most are female. Corporate America has opened its doors (somewhat) to a whole new generation of well-educated, well-qualified African Americans. All of these facts contribute to the possibilities that present themselves to Black couples and families. So we've come a long way, baby!

But what we see on television (owned, managed, and produced by White America) and read about in books (primarily written by White men and women) is not reality to the masses of Black Americans. Sure, a few of us are doing well, very well. We've got the home in the suburbs and the kids in private school, and we take a vacation in the Caribbean once a year.

But a home in the burbs is not the reality for the majority of the 33.9 million Black Americans. And it's not because they're not smart. Let's face it, wouldn't you have to be smart and ambitious and creative to survive the mean streets of Chicago, Detroit, or New York? But for a multitude of reasons—some of them known, some unknown—they're stuck where they are, the result of second- or third-generation disillusioned Black men and women stuck on a treadmill of undereducation, unemployment, crime, neglect, despair, and all the other evils born out of poverty and the burden of color.

The history and severity of the race problem in America has had a profound impact on our search for mates. The leaders of this nation would have us believe that this country of freemen doesn't owe Black people anything. They are convinced that this nation has done all it can do to help Black people help themselves. They believe that Black people, in general, are shiftless and lazy and prefer to live in broken-down, rat-infested, graffiti-covered, ten-story tenements in urban America. According to the powers that be, anybody ought to be able to pull themselves up by their bootstraps (assuming they have boots!). After all, aren't thirty years of civil rights legislation enough to right the wrongs of 244 years of chains and shackles and beatings and rapes and hangings and another hundred years of the Klan and Jim Crow and Strom Thurmond and Ronald Reagan?

The answer is no. A resounding no! If you are uneducated, unskilled, unemployed, trapped in the poverty and despair of urban ghettos, it's hard to think of anything but surviving another day the best way you can. Sometimes it means getting out, but often it means getting over. It's called survival. Too many of our brothers feel helpless and hopeless and do not see a way out. Those few who manage to find a way out sometimes find it difficult to cope in a world where they are still overwhelmingly judged by the color of their skin, the size of their lips, and the shape of their nose. This can make it difficult for them to think about committing to anything but themselves. Marriage and providing for a family may be too permanent. It's far easier to hit and run. A woman here. A baby there. No responsibilities. No strings.

Before you start throwing stones at me for making excuses for Black men, get a grip! I don't make excuses for grown men with choices. I'm mad at a lot of my brothers. I hate the fact that many of them are taking the easy way out by being stupid and cowardly and victimizing their own people. An example of this is beating Rosa Parks and leaving her for dead. I'm mad at them for being seduced by drugs and alcohol and making addicts and criminals out of the women and children who are trapped with them in the inner cities.

I resent the fact that Black men are dropping semen all over America and don't seem to care that their sperm may produce real-life human beings in nine months. I hate the fact that young sisters can't seem to see beyond our brothers' cute little behinds and say no to these predators who have no intention of making a commitment to them or their children. I'm disappointed that too many of our kids are growing up poor, on public assistance, in single-parent homes, without benefit of positive male role models.

At the same time, though, I understand that the responsibility for some of these conditions has to be shared with White America. Can you imagine putting your foot on someone's back for 346 years—from the arrival of the first boatload of slaves in 1619 to the height of the modern-day civil rights movement in 1965—and then taking your foot off and telling him to stand up and walk like a man . . . talk like a man . . . act like a man? Then a mere thirty years later wondering why "they" haven't caught up with civilized people (translation: White folks); wondering why "they" can't seem to control themselves and not be seduced by the drugs that somebody (I wonder who?) seems to be slipping into their communities; wondering why they can't seem to keep their "thing" in their pants and stop making so many babies, when making healthy little baby slaves was a full-time job for our men for more than 200 years (this sounds like selective memory to me!).

While White America was passing down a tradition of motherhood and apple pie, our great-grandmothers were teaching their kids how to accept being separated from their mothers and fathers and sisters and brothers. They were teaching our sisters to accept having their bodies ravished by anyone in authority. Our boys and men were learning to determine their value by how often they used their thing to reproduce for the massa.

It is no wonder that so many of our men still gauge their value by the number of babies they can make. It is no mystery that so many of our young women do not respect themselves or their bodies. Bad or good, traditions die hard. Slavery did more than just enslave our bodies. We are imprisoned by invisible chains and shackles of self-hate, self-doubt, and feelings of inferiority. These emotions have replaced physical chains and are just as real to millions of Black Americans.

This reality includes the fact that we arrived in America on the bottom of slave ships and were forced to live subhuman lives for the next two hundred years in a country built on our blood, sweat, and tears. This reality makes it ludicrous to believe that we could ever truly compete with the White man on a level playing field—in any arena. I know we've always been good, very good at imitating White folks. I've read about the house slaves turning on the field slaves during slavery, the mulattoes denying their darker-skinned brothers and sisters during Reconstruction. And let's not forget the twentieth-century bourgeoisie desperately trying to ignore the plight of the Black underclass.

At some point, we must stop the masquerade. Racism, unfortunately, is here to stay . . . like fast food, computers, and Volvos. The fact is that we are never going to get our forty acres and a mule. However, we still have to go on. We are going to have to look past the issue of race and become concerned about an issue that we can do something about. An issue that we have neglected for a very long time: the Black family.

Too many Black men and women have been so concerned (even obsessed) with the issue of race that we have neglected resulting problems facing African Americans. It's not rednecks with shotguns in pickup trucks (although I've met a few face-to-face on a dark street and lived to talk about it). It's not the Newt Gingriches or Clarence Thomases. It's not the death of affirmative action. It is the death of the Black family.

The Black family starts with Black men and Black women, and that's where *we* have to start. We have to learn how to talk to one another about family and values. We need to talk about our relationships. We need to discuss keeping Black men and women together to build better families and communities and to raise more emotionally and intellectually equipped children.

We cannot continue to walk in the shadows of a lie—a lie that says that, because there is a history of oppression and racism in this country that has treated us cruelly, we must treat one another cruelly. We cannot continue to allow pride and selfishness and overinflated egos to sabotage our relationships with one another and then blame White America as we lie and cheat and beat one another out of our dignity, self-respect, and stereos. We also cannot afford to lose another generation of young people because far too many brothers refuse to grow up and father the children they help create.

We can't be afraid to redefine what *family* means in our community. We should not be fooled by what we think the ideal family should look like—father, mother, 2.5 kids, house in the suburbs. We need to concentrate on what the Black family really is for the majority of Black Americans.

In our families, we have 67 percent of Black children growing up in homes without fathers. We have children who are being raised by mostly poor, uneducated, unskilled single mothers. Single mothers who are sixteen or twenty-six or forty-six who continue to make life choices about men and love and sex that adversely affect them, Black families, and ultimately Black America. Most often these women's self-worth is inextricably tied into whether they have someone to warm their bed on Friday and help buy groceries on Monday. These women give men permission to bed them and break them, all in the same week. They also believe they are nothing and could never be anything without a man in their life.

This book was written for these women and for countless other single Black women (with or without children) who need to be reminded that they have a right—a God-given right—to a happy, satisfying, fulfilling life without a constant fear of being abandoned, abused, neglected, and misused by the opposite sex. We have to learn ways that we can encourage and support one another so all of us can make better choices about the men we allow to come into our lives and our beds. Learning to say "no" and "no more" takes a lot of courage, but Black women wrote the book on courage! We are survivors. I have no doubt that we'll survive the crisis facing Black relationships, Black families, and Black America today.

3

What Women Want

"More things belong in marriage than four bare legs in bed."

I don't know what all women want! If I could answer that, I'd be sipping Dom Pérignon from 24K gold–rimmed glasses and lighting the fireplace with hundred-dollar bills on the Ivory Coast or the French Riviera.

What do I *think* most of us want? First and foremost, we want a man. Not just any man, mind you, *our* man. The man that was promised to us when we were little girls dreaming of ways to move away from home or get out of the projects. We are looking for Mr. Right—not Mr. Right Now. He doesn't have to be perfect, but he should be perfect for us. We imagine someone with the looks of an African prince, the character and courage of a knight in shining armor, the strength of Samson, the passion of Romeo, and the fidelity of the Pope (Please, God!).

What self-respecting woman wouldn't want all of that—and then some—rolled into one man? Yet most reasonably intelligent women realize that such men don't grow on trees (they certainly don't grow on the trees in my neighborhood). And in all likelihood, they don't exist except in our schoolgirl dreams.

We yearn for someone to love us and need us and protect us. We hope we'll meet someone we can depend on to bring home at least some of the bacon some of the time. Someone who doesn't beat us, brand us, or blame us when things go wrong. A man who understands that nobody owns you, no matter how much they might invest in you. Someone who wants to make us happy in and out of bed. Our man should enjoy being with us before, during, and after sex and get as excited about the "journey" as he does about the "destination" (think about it!). We want a man to whom we can give all this love we've been saving for so many years.

We also want a good sex life. (There, I said it!) Contrary to popular belief, most of us like s-e-x. We like *good* s-e-x. We don't like slam-bam-thank-you-ma'am sex (excuse me, are you finished already?) or look-at-me-see-what-I-just-did sex (and what is it exactly that you think you did?). Most of us want someone who knows the difference between love and lust, between making love and having sex. We want a man who understands that although some women occasionally enjoy having sex with someone they love, most of us prefer making love with someone we're having sex with. (Try to keep up, please!)

In the real world, what we have are men who are reasonably attractive, reasonably intelligent, reasonably ambitious, reasonably romantic, and, thank God, reasonably sane. Since most of us fall within this same zone of reasonableness, we should make perfect couples.

So why don't we? One reason may be that women want quality and men want quantity. Too many men are concerned about the chase and the kill. Most women are concerned about the morning after. (To brothers reading this book: Don't get mad. If it doesn't apply to you, I'm not referring to you!) I know I'm generalizing, but that doesn't mean there's not some truth in it. Since 1986, I've talked to thousands of Black women all over the country. Women from all walks of life. Career women. Welfare mothers. College students. Grandmothers. Women in recovery. I've discovered, not surprisingly, that most of these women share the same hopes and dreams that I do. Most of us want the basics—health, wealth, and happiness—and we'd like to share it with one person. We are looking for a companion whom we can love, trust, and respect. A man who brings more than an erection to the relationship, one who is sensitive and warm and caring and understanding and supportive. We want someone who can feel love and sorrow and pity and is not embarrassed to express it.

Most of us want someone who doesn't make all of his decisions from his waist down. We want someone who knows that if he shows us just a little love and respect, he won't have to swindle us out of sex. We want someone who takes his time and cares if and when we get "ours." And when we don't get ours, we want someone who will take the time to make sure we do before he lights up a cancer stick or falls asleep.

We want a man who appreciates the strength, courage, and tenacity of Black women and doesn't need a White woman to massage his ego and feed his insecurities. We want someone who has at least a sprinkling of ambition and doesn't mind working for a living. After all, if I get up and go to work every day, then so should every grown person in the house! We want someone who doesn't worship material wealth but understands that money does have a place in a healthy, happy relationship (it's hard to be happy as a pig in a pen when you're cold, hungry, homeless, and in debt up to your navel).

We want a companion who appreciates our friendship and isn't driven to spending three or four nights a week with the boys in order to find someone who "understands" and "appreciates" him. We want a teacher—someone who is willing to share the things that he enjoys, such as sports and cars, in an attempt to bring us closer together. We want someone who is receptive to learning how to sew a button on the shirt he has to wear, make the bed he slept in, and cook the casserole he's going to eat. We want someone who knows that "fetching" and "carrying" (e.g., the paper, the remote control, a glass of water) is a two-way street. Women who work eight- or ten-hour days don't mind occasionally fetching and carrying if we know that someone will occasionally fetch and carry for us.

Frankly, we want someone who is tired of little-boy games of pursue and conquer, who can control his roving eye, who doesn't feel that he needs a different woman every time he takes in a fresh supply of oxygen. We want a man who doesn't have to be taught that honesty is the best policy and that the best way to destroy a decent relationship is to lie and screw around. We want a man who is not threatened by material things that we might possess when we first meet him—a job, a car, a house—because he knows that all of us are a paycheck away from the unemployment line. We want a man who is secure enough to applaud our accomplishments and share our successes. We prefer someone who not only encourages us to be the best but brings out the best in us.

What do women want? Simply to love and be loved by someone who wants to love and be loved. We want the same thing the marines want—just a few good men.

4

What Women Need

"Women have to be and feel no more than what they are and no less than what they must be."

Regardless of what men think, most women simply want and need the truth. I don't know who started the vicious rumor that women prefer to be lied to. I don't think you're going to find too many of us who will confess that we look forward to men lying to us. Yes, even when it hurts, boyfriend, we need the truth! Certainly not to the exclusion of everything else (like love, understanding, loyalty, emotional support, and companionship), but the truth is a good place to start.

Either you want us or you don't. Either you want to make it work or you don't. Either you're here for a quickie or you're here for the long haul. Just tell us the truth—not half-truths, not distortions, and definitely not your *version* of the truth. If you were to tell us the truth, you might be surprised when we do not throw ourselves out of a window just because you tell us that it's over. Some of us might not slash your tires (or your throat) or spray-paint your BMW if you have the courage to tell us that you're seeing someone else (especially if it's someone named Steve). We might thank you for saving our lives. After all, in this age of HIV and AIDS, it's not a good idea to drop your drawers for someone who's dropping his for more than one person at a time.

We want the truth and nothing but the truth. If you ask a thousand women what has caused the most pain and grief in their relationships, don't be surprised if they list lies, lies, and more lies. For a lot of women, honesty ranks right up there with love and respect when it comes to priorities in a relationship. How often have we heard a girlfriend say, "How can you love a man you can't trust?" Too many times have we let the little white lies slide because we're in love. Because of love we make excuses for behavior that should be inexcusable. We pretend that we're blind and stupid, wading through lie after lie because we think we're in love. Even Stevie Wonder could see your man's cheating, but we ignore it in the name of love.

If you ask men why they lie, this is what some of them will tell you: "I didn't want to hurt the woman's feelings." "I wanted to avoid a confrontation." "I didn't want to end the relationship until I made sure the new one was going to work out." "I thought I could get away with it." Whatever the reason (or excuse) men give for lying, after a while the lies all begin to sound alike. What do men lie about? How do you spell E-V-E-R-Y-T-H-I-N-G? Here are a few examples of what we let them get away with:

1. "I'm not married!" We believe him even though we can see the imprint of a wedding band on the third finger of his left hand and guilt is dripping off his brow into his Courvoisier like purple rain.

2. "I don't remember how this lipstick got on my collar! I think my secretary slipped down a flight of steps today and I

caught her." There are eight sets of lip prints on his shirt and his shorts. Maybe he should think about having the tramp see a brain surgeon or a good chiropractor.

3. "You know I love you, Baby!" This may or may not be the truth, depending on the time, place, and how much heat he's in. Have you noticed these six words are frequently used while he's screwing you or after he's screwed up?

4. "I don't know who she is, Baby!" A man may say this after he and some hussy have danced seven times in a row and you've gotten wallpaper sores from standing in a corner fighting off rejects with bad breath at a party in a dump that you didn't want to go to in the first place. He may not have known who she was when she came in but you can bet her fake Gucci bag, polyester pants, and vinyl shoes that he'll know her name, number, and sun sign before she leaves.

5. "This has never happened to me before, Baby!" This remark may come after an unfortunate attempt to get it on one night. Give us a break! He's not the first guy who couldn't get (or keep) an erection and he won't be the last. It happens! If he has a problem, talk about it. You're a big girl. If you care about him, you can take the truth. If you start laughing hysterically, he shouldn't be with you in the first place. Relax. Talk about it. Try again later. He doesn't have to lie about it!

6. "I'll call you tonight/tomorrow/next week" (pick one). This is a classic. It's got to be in the *Guinness Book of World Records* under the most-used lie! These four words are usually spoken minutes after you've made out and, more often than not, at your home in your bed. Men rarely say this when you leave them alone in their bed the morning after. I suspect that there's something about being in their own domain that makes them feel that they don't have to promise anybody anything.

7. "I'm sorry I'm late. I stopped by a friend's house right after

work and he didn't have a phone!" Mind you, he got off work at 6 P.M. and came home after 2 A.M. So you have a friend who doesn't have a phone. What is he, the Neanderthal man? (If you're going to lie, at least try to be creative.)

8. "I'm going to get some cigarettes. I'll be back in a few minutes." Four hours later, he strolls in, empty-handed and smelling like a distillery, and wonders why you're fuming!

9. This is my favorite: "It's not what you think. She doesn't mean a thing to me. You're overreacting!" He says this after you've caught him having a drink in a bar with a half-naked girl thirty miles from home at four in the afternoon; or, God forbid, after you've caught him in your bed with a fully naked girl when you came home from work early one day.

The list goes on and on. The almighty lie. What can we do about it? Unfortunately, not much. People lie. Men (and women) will lie to you as often as they can, especially if they think they're getting away with it. The secret is to build a relationship that doesn't permit too many untruths to creep in and start chipping away at the foundation. When the foundation is weak, it's easy for people to get hurt. Solid relationships are built from the ground up by two committed people who care enough about the relationship that purposely hurting each other is not an option. And no matter how you look at it, lies hurt. Lies rob us of the love, respect, and trust that relationships must be built on to survive. Relationships have a better chance of surviving when both partners are open and honest about their feelings, desires, and expectations; when they don't keep secrets from each other; and when they can be depended on to *say* what they mean and *mean* what they say. Since a lot of us don't have those kinds of relationships (if we did, do you think we'd need this book?), perhaps we should start looking at the cost we all pay for our lack of trust.

First, if you expect most people to be straight with you (and a lot of women do), you must accept the fact that telling the truth is still a novel experience for a lot of men (I didn't say ALL!). Habitual liars think that (1) we believe everything they tell us and (2) they won't get caught. Based on these two assumptions, we can safely deduce that habitual liars suffer from an overdose of self-confidence. We should be as confident as they are that we won't be enslaved by liars or their self-serving lies.

We should have zero tolerance for liars. I know it's difficult because when you care about someone, you want to believe everything he says. A lie is a deliberate attempt to deceive someone. You are the only person who can decide whether you can live with the deception. We are not responsible for how, when, or if people hurt us, but we are responsible for how we respond to the hurt. You don't have to be a garbage disposal for lies. If you know beyond a shadow of a doubt you've been deceived and your relationship is suffering, confront him. Even if he denies it, if you don't believe him and don't think you can ever forgive him, move on. Do not hesitate. It'll take more courage to walk away from him than to stay with him—not believing, not trusting, not quite loving him the same anymore.

The wounds of a broken relationship can heal; the pain will pass and you will survive. It's difficult to love someone you don't trust, since true love and trust are inseparable. When you're crying yourself into a coma during the first couple of weeks after giving him his walking papers, remind yourself that relationships don't work for people who don't want to work for them. Even if you momentarily believed he was Mr. Right, if you couldn't trust him, you're better off without him!

5

Some Things Mother Never Told Us

"Being male is a matter of birth. Being a man is a matter of choice."

As painful as it is to admit, we still live in a sexist society. Prejudice and discrimination against women are evident in everything from wages to protection from domestic violence and sexual assault. In this society there are unwritten rules about women. For many men (who still write the rules), the logical progression in a woman's life is:

1. BIRTH: Remember when baby girls used to be a major disappointment to the whole tribe?
2. SCHOOL: To learn how to read cookbooks.
3. MARRIAGE: To give him a legal and steady dose of you-know-what.
4. MOTHERHOOD: To prove his sperm are virile.
5. SAINT: When he starts playing around.
6. MARTYR: When he dies and leaves no life insurance.
7. DEATH: The inevitable end, usually a blessing after fifty or sixty years of numbers 1 through 6.

Here are a few facts our mothers should have told us but didn't about being a woman. It's not their fault they didn't tell us. No one ever told them: Their grandmothers were too busy breast-feeding Miss Sally's young'uns; their great-grandmothers were too busy picking cotton or scrubbing Miss Ann's floors. But it's never too late to learn:

1. You don't have to play the I-don't-have-a-man-woe-is-me blues. You don't have to feel illegitimate without a man. If you do, it's because you want to. You are a child of the living God—a thinking, breathing child of God with your own soul and a heart that beats independently of anyone else. Understandably, after years of misdirected energy and childish dreams, there is a real conflict brewing between wanting to be independent and wanting to have a man whom you can depend on (at least some of the time).

The reality is that we cannot afford to allow the fear of being alone to indefinitely retard our growth as human beings. Fear of being alone is not uncommon but it is unnecessary. Most of us come into this world alone (unless you're a twin) and will die alone (unless you're in a tragic plane accident). We have to understand that sometime between birth and death, we're going to be alone. It's inevitable (unless you've got a full-time imaginary friend).

Too many of us feel that if we don't constantly have someone in our lives to validate our existence we are nothing. This belief reinforces the desperate, panic-stricken, love-deprived-single-woman stereotype. I see it in the faces of women all across this nation. I hear it in their voices. I see it in their tears. The truth is that there's not always going to be someone around to love us and hug us and make us feel good about ourselves—even if we're married. If you don't believe me, ask a few of your married friends to tell you the truth. They may have husbands, but many of them still feel alone and lonely. They may even admit that they yearn for our lives, what they perceive as the life of a swinging single. The grass always looks greener on the other side—that's human nature. The key to fulfillment is to be able to enjoy what you have. To learn how to accept what is here and now in your life. To be content in whatever state you're in until *you're* willing and ready to change it.

Learning to love ourselves should be at the top of our list of priorities. When we learn that self-love is not conceit—that it is not a luxury—we will be one step closer to learning to love someone else. Also, when you feel good about yourself, it's easier to accept love (if it's good for you) and reject love (if it's not so good for you). If you're confident and secure with who you are and your place in the universe, then it's even easier. But, if you feel bad about yourself, *no* man can make you feel good. I don't care how fine he is—or how fine *he* thinks he is.

2. Mother never told us that it's okay to enjoy s-e-x. (There. I said it again.) Maybe no one talked about sex in your home. Maybe your mother didn't know enough about it to tell you about it. Maybe she didn't enjoy it. I don't know why so many mothers are reluctant to sit down with their daughters and have a heart-to-heart about sex. Perhaps if some of us could have talked about sex when we were growing up, it would have been easier for us to distinguish sex from love later on.

Love is spelled l-o-v-e. *Sex* is spelled l-u-s-t. Sometimes people in love have sex. But more often, people in lust have sex. These two words, *love* and *lust*, are not interchangeable. Too many of us equate sex with love. If we have sex with someone, we think that the intimacy of the moment automatically creates the foundation for a solid relationship. More often than not, we find the opposite to be true. It was a nice moment (or two) but he may not be ready to make a commitment—except maybe to find out the next time you can get together to have sex.

We're amazed that the man we just made love to doesn't want us, and doesn't want to spend quality time with us. After all, didn't he just see us naked? Didn't we just share spit and a bed? Maybe that's your answer why he doesn't want to see you again. While most women are looking for love and romance and believe that sex is what you do to get it, most of the men we meet seem to be looking for sex . . . period. Men know that love and romance is what they must provide in order to get sex. What most men won't (not don't) realize is that the best sex in the world is with someone you care about and someone who cares about you. If you're lucky, they're the same person.

Men and women are on different pages in the same book because we're not communicating. Either we don't know how to communicate with each other or we don't have the courage to tell the people we care about what we want and need from them, including good sex. Why aren't we communicating effectively? Sometimes, out of fear of rejection or abandonment, we've become so accustomed to saying and doing what we *think* other people want us to say and do that we've lost our identity, grown numb to our own needs, and don't know what we want. We're afraid to say what we really mean or ask for what we really want. Other times we don't communicate because we don't want to be honest and bare our souls to men who won't commit to more than one night. Maybe we don't communicate because we think that we don't deserve more than one-night stands and bad sex.

For the record, *sex* is not a dirty word. It's a natural and often pleasurable release of energy. But for many of us brought up in Christian homes (that would be most Black women), trying to be obedient to our religious beliefs while trying to satisfy our physical and emotional needs makes it especially difficult to have men moving in and out of our beds at regular—or even irregular—intervals. This continuous motion can be still more traumatic if we don't have a healthy attitude toward sex or realistic expectations about "living happily ever after" with the person we happen to be bedding at the time.

Many of us Christian girls in our thirties or forties or fifties were taught that fornicating (polite language) is morally wrong and socially unacceptable. After all, didn't God create sex to populate the earth within the boundaries of marriage? Thus, fornicating with a new person every year (sometimes every few months, depending on your track record) ensures us a seat in hell next to Jeffrey Dahmer. We usually justify these bouts of physical intimacy by saying, "I know I said I wasn't going to get involved with someone who wasn't interested in a long-term exclusive relationship, but *this* time it's going to be different." And while you're waiting for it to be different, you wake up, he's gone, the pipe dream is over and you resign yourself to being alone, again, maybe forever. Kind of sad, isn't it?

Why do we fall into the same trap over and over again? Why do bright, intelligent, educated women have such a difficult time identifying lust and distinguishing it from love? Perhaps because many of us still look at sex as a gift that we give to men in exchange for services rendered. Three-for-one drinks at happy hour. A superficial conversation over dinner at a hole-in-the-wall. One phone call following the initial act.

We have to acknowledge that we play a role in encouraging this kind of behavior. We have to stop hopping into bed with someone just because he's spent a few dollars on popcorn and a movie. Regardless of what he may think, we don't owe him anything but a polite "thank you." Sex should not be sold or bartered for a three-dollar cheeseburger or a thirty-dollar steak. After a pleasant evening out, thank the brother, kiss him (if you want to), and say good night. If he never calls back, consider yourself lucky that you found out sooner, rather than later, that he was only interested in sex.

It's not that we don't have physical needs. Most of us enjoy sex and would enjoy it even more if we had better sex. But we shouldn't settle for sex if we want something more. The same way we take responsibility for what we eat for breakfast or wear to work, we must learn to take responsibility for our sexual choices. I'm talking about taking responsibility for making sure that we enjoy the physical relationships we get involved in and that we're not pressured into sex just because someone else has decided that it's time to do it. On the other hand, taking responsibility means sometimes taking the initiative when we meet someone we're interested in. Where is it written that we always have to sit back and wait for someone else to choose us or call us? Actually, we should all be waiting for God to choose someone for us. But since most of us insist on giving God a little help—whether he wants it or not—why don't *we* choose for a change?

Choosing means trusting our instincts and intuition, our inner spirit, our inner voice. More often than not, our instincts will keep us from going too far left or right, particularly if we are in tune with the Creator of the universe. In other words, if a man looks and acts like a creep, he's probably a creep. If he looks and acts too good to be true, he probably is. If you get a sense that you ought to at least give a man a second look, give him a second look.

Trusting our intuition doesn't mean we're always going to make good choices. Sometimes we're *still* going to play the fool. There are a lot of charlatans and sociopaths out there. If we're in tune with our basic instincts of right and wrong, good and bad, and don't let loneliness and desperation cloud our vision, our instincts will very seldom steer us wrong. It's when we wage war against our instincts and do exactly the opposite of what our heart and soul are telling us to do that we get in trouble. Think about the last time you ignored your gut feeling about someone—the doubt, the hesitation, the questions. Think about the aftermath. I wasn't even there but I can tell you it wasn't a pretty picture, was it?

The truth is that the less we ignore those little red flags that go up when we are getting ready to do something stupid, the more successful we become in the selection process. Success breeds confidence. And in-your-face-confidence is what we've got to have if we're ever going to get what we want and need from the men that we meet—and that includes a satisfying sex life.

Taking responsibility also means having the courage to give directions to someone who may be lost on the road to your gratification. I don't mean sitting in bed with a map and a flashlight saying, "here, there, slower, faster, to the right, to the left, hip, hut." I mean being mature enough to discuss what makes you happy in bed and gently guiding him to mutual gratification. Psychologists say you shouldn't discuss the issue at that very moment. Okay. Fine. But unless you want to spend the next twenty years of your life giving and not getting, you had better learn sign language or learn to speak up.

Here's the bottom line: If you are going to sweat (I said sweat not perspire) for twenty minutes (and that's being generous), mess up your hair, and miss *Nightline*, the least you can do is enjoy it. If you're involved in a physical relationship and you're afraid it might shatter his ego to tell him that you'd rather count lint on an old sweater than make love, you deserve what you get (or don't get). Very seldom do men leave unsatisfied; why should we?

3. Another thing that Mother never told us (God bless her heart!) is that we don't have to start looking through the Yellow

Pages for a wedding consultant every time we sleep with someone (who sleeps?). Will it last more than one night? We don't know. Is it going to lead to a relationship or marriage or kids? We don't know. Since we can't predict the future or see around corners, sometimes we have to trust our instincts and take a chance on love. If you tried to change your personality every time a new person entered your life, you'd be schizophrenic. You wouldn't need a date—you'd need a caretaker!

Wait a minute! I'm reading your mind: You think it's going to be hard to enjoy yourself if there is a possibility that he won't call again. News flash: There's *always* that possibility! Although most of us prefer to engage in LWP (lust with potential), there are no guarantees that the people we sleep with are ever going to call again. Plan B: If the object of your affection doesn't call again, call him. If he doesn't return your call, forget him. As soon as you can accept the fact that he's not your Prince Charming, the sooner you can let go of the regret. Stop whining and complaining about how he "done you wrong" and get on with your life. You can't make people love you. You can't make them stay. They love you for their own reasons. They stay or leave for their own reasons. We love them for our own reasons. When we make a mistake and give our hearts to the wrong person, we must learn to forgive ourselves. We must learn to move on by showing ourselves compassion. If he never calls again, realize it might be a blessing in disguise. You should thank the Lord for sparing you five or six months—or more—of unnecessary pain and agony of loving someone who doesn't love you and never had any real intention of fulfilling your wildest dreams!

Unfortunately, there is no foolproof way to weed out the men who want only a one-night stand from the ones who want an open, honest, lasting relationship. Many of our men are so protective of their emotions and so careful not to reveal who they really are that what they say and do are in direct conflict with each other. He may whisper sweet nothings in your ear for two weeks straight and then never call again. He may send cards and flowers to your office every day for a month, sleep with you one Friday night, and then disappear, never to be heard from again. Here too, there are no guarantees.

If we can't tell the good guys from the bad guys, what should we do? How do we make sure that we don't wind up in a series of unfulfilling affairs (as opposed to relationships) that leave us emotionally chained to feelings of guilt, confusion, and hopelessness?

First, don't knock a little confusion and guilt. Both of them can help us learn valuable lessons—sometimes the hard way. *Love* and *sex* are on different pages in the dictionary. They're two different words with two different meanings. Unfortunately for a lot of us, learning the difference hasn't been easy or fun. After our share of con artists, chameleons, sexual derelicts, and other forgettables through the years, many of us want to give up our search for love. Regrettably, we find out that there are men you should follow anywhere *but* the bedroom. We also find out that even some of those you do follow to the bedroom, you shouldn't always sleep with.

As we pursue our pursuer, too many of them are usually in pursuit of pure and simple pleasure—immediate gratification—without a second thought to our emotional well-being. Even those of us who think we can "be adult about sex" without becoming too promiscuous—i.e., give him a "little" to get him interested and then pray he comes back for more—may soon begin to have doubts about our decision to participate in the sexual revolution.

We find out that most of us simply are not designed that way. Most of us do not have the love-'em-and-leave-'em instinct. We discover that hopping in and out of beds, hoping to find the right bed—the *lifetime* bed—is a waste of perfectly good time and energy. We learn that unless you're extremely careful, it's easy to get on a never-ending merry-go-round of dead-end affairs that leave you feeling even more confused, guilty, and hopeless.

In an ideal world, sex without benefit of marriage would be unthinkable. In the real world, however, men and women who are not married sometimes take off their clothes and have sex with each other. Right or wrong. Good or bad. It happens. And when it does, marriage is not always the destination.

The most important thing we can remember is something that the Isley Brothers wrote a song about a few years ago. Actually, it's something that a few of our mothers did tell us: "It's Your Thang!" You heard me. It may be crude, it may be rude. But it's the truth. It *is* our thing and as soon as we stop thinking that giving up control of "our thing" to someone is the only way we are going to find (and keep) Mr. Right, the sooner we can get on with creating a satisfying life—with or without him.

The sooner we realize that if and when we have sex, it should be because we want to have sex and not because we think it may lead to something. Sometimes it does and sometimes it doesn't. Either way, it's still our thing and we get to choose. I repeat: With choice comes responsibility. When we choose to have sex, it is our responsibility to accept the fact that we may be giving some child in man's clothes—suffering from emotional paralysis every time he finds himself more than just a little attached to a woman—the right to victimize us. After we have sex, we must restrain ourselves from immediately sitting down to write a fairy tale with a happy ending for a man who may be unable—and, more importantly, unwilling—to commit. Every time we choose to have sex, we must expect the unexpected—reality—to overrule the ideal.

Your decision to experience sex without a promise of love or marriage is just that—your decision. Some of us can do it effortlessly. Some of us cannot. Regardless of how you use sex, your ultimate goal should be to place yourself in an environment that keeps you in control of your body and your soul. If you are willing to accept crumbs, there will always be someone coming in and out of your life (and your bed) who will insist on giving you crumbs. If you want a whole slice of bread, you must say no to the crumbs.

You must say no to occasional late-night visits from "vampires" who never call you during daylight hours but expect you to be ready when they decide that they have time for you—between 1:00 and 1:07 A.M. on the second Tuesday before the full moon of the third month of the leap year following the Olympics.

If you want the whole slice, get to know someone before you hop into his bed on the first date because he "smelled so good." If he gets the milk and the cow on his first visit to the farm, why should he come back?

Sex without marriage won't cause insanity, sterility, or pregnancy every time. But that doesn't mean that we get up and walk away unaffected. You must be willing to take responsibility for the choices—good and bad—that you make in your quest to find Mr. Right. Accept the challenge and take charge of your own life, your own happiness, and your own destiny. Most importantly, stop feeling, acting, looking, walking, talking, and living like a victim.

6

Taking Charge

"Life is what happens while you're making other plans."

I wrote this book for two very selfish reasons. First, I was concerned about my future—unattached—and my continued personal growth and happiness if I remained unmarried. Second, I'd like to make a couple of million dollars, retire, and move to the Virgin Islands (don't get mad at me 'cause I'm honest!).

Okay. So I had a few altruistic reasons as well. I wrote this book to share what I believe are the answers to some of the most devastating problems that haunt single women in their search for Mr. Right. I am on a personal mission to stop single women from wasting even one precious moment of their one solitary life waiting for that perfect relationship to materialize, always looking for someone to come into their lives, rescue them and make them whole.

I'd like to be a cheerleader for women who are as tired of settling as I am. Women who are learning that if we settle for something less today and something different tomorrow, what will we settle for next week, next month, next year? Beautiful, intelligent sisters who have more choices than they realize and must learn to cherish and accept responsibility for those choices. We must understand that our pursuit of happiness begins and ends with the choices we make in our everyday lives.

If you didn't skip the first few chapters, you have probably already noticed that I talk a lot about sex. No, I'm not preoccupied with the subject of sex, but I do believe that many of the problems we face as single women searching for Mr. Right stem from the lessons we have been taught (or not taught) about sex and sexuality.

As I travel across the United States as a motivational speaker and trainer, I talk and listen to thousands of women, mostly African American women, about the trials and tribulations of being Black and female in a country that has little regard for either group. More often than not, the subject turns to love and relationships and marriage and, ultimately, sex. Why? Traditionally, women have viewed sex as something sacred—to be brought out, dressed up, and given away on Valentine's Day or Christmas. Or dusted off and presented as an afternoon delight for men who—by their mere presence in our lives—have earned it and therefore deserve it.

If you don't already know that nobody deserves it unless you want to give it to them, then I'm really glad you bought this book. Sex is a gift to mankind (and womankind) from God. Your body is the temple of God. It belongs to you, and no one has the right to abuse or misuse it. When you allow other people to come into your life and take charge of your body—or your emotions—even for a short period of time, you have given up the most important God-given right you possess: your right to choose.

Unfortunately, many women find it difficult to exercise their right to choose, to say yes or no and mean it. We're afraid to let our voices be heard, particularly about our sexuality. At thirty or forty or even fifty years old, some of us are still afraid to openly acknowledge our body and physical desires for fear that someone (our men, maybe our mothers), might conclude that we really do enjoy sex. We do enjoy sex. And we would enjoy it even more if men would become more skillful lovers and take the time to satisfy our needs as readily as they tend to theirs.

Keep in mind that men are not on trial here. Their lovemaking skills are not under investigation. If we're not satisfied with our relationships—physically, emotionally, intellectually—and we choose to do or say nothing about it, we deserve what we get! Even babies ask for what they want. They communicate their needs and desires in a hundred different ways. So why are adult women so afraid to speak up? Why are we afraid to speak the truth in love?

The problem is very complex. We may be unhappy and dissatisfied with the relationship that we're in, but so many of us are even more afraid to be alone that we'll do whatever it takes not to be. Maybe we don't want to take responsibility for our own mental health and happiness, so we tolerate the thoughtlessness, the inconsideration, the disrespect. Perhaps we don't speak up because we are afraid that they will run from us and the truth, that they can't handle the truth. The truth is that we deserve more. If we don't expect—or demand—more, we'll never get it.

And then there's the shame and guilt of several hundred years of being told that we don't deserve more. After all, we're the descendants of Africans. Real Africans from Africa. We are as beautiful and shapely and sensuous as our proud ancestors were, and yet we have become obsessed with the European standard of beauty: Five foot six, 106 pounds, size 6 dress, size 6 shoe size, six-inch waist, six-inch bust. Some of us are ashamed of our bodies if we have a few extra pounds here and there, particularly if we are well-endowed in the hip and thigh areas. We are forever trying to force our size 12 or 14 frames into size 6 designer jeans that obviously were not cut for us (Gloria Vanderbilt even told us that!).

In a nation of more than 260 million Americans, of different sizes, shapes, and colors, it's impossible to have one standard of beauty. Yet many of us allow the media (driven by skinny fashion models and designers) to define what's acceptable and what's not. We measure our self-worth and desirability by the shape of our nose or what size dress we wear. Our unwillingness to accept our African features has created a generation of dissatisfaction—with our bodies and ourselves. Our struggle with issues of self-esteem and self-worth makes us a magnet for men who do not appreciate our unique style and beauty and take advantage of our desire to be in somebody else's body. When we don't respect and honor our bodies and who we are apart from our bodies, neither do they.

Have we forgotten the unique beauty and spirit of the African woman, stolen from her native land and forced to breed a nation of survivors? Have we forgotten that our near-perfect breasts, bountiful hips, and caramel complexion are envied all around the world (except perhaps here in America?). If we cannot learn to accept and love ourselves as descendants of full-figured African queens and high priestesses from the motherland, we will never be able to accept and love anyone else.

When our men refuse to accept our bodies as fifth- or sixth-generation African women, then they deny their own heritage. They deny their own thick noses; full lips; ashy skin; unsightly razor bumps; thin, unshapely but strong legs; and—I might add—their tight, curved little bee-hinds. Learning to appreciate our unique cultural and physical differences frees us to fully express our sexuality. To feel comfortable with our bodies—generous supply of flesh and all. It means choosing to speak up when it just ain't happening for us under the sheets. It means becoming less inhibited about asking for what we want and deserve in the privacy of our own (or someone else's) bedroom. In a nutshell, it simply means taking charge of your life and identifying, asking for, and getting what you want—including love!

7

What Is Love?

"You can give without loving but you cannot love without giving."

Love. What is it? I wish I knew. The experts have been trying to define it for years. *Webster's* defines *love*, the noun, as "strong affection . . . tenderness . . . warm attachment . . . or devotion." *Love* is also a verb. It's not just a feeling, or something that you *say*. It's something that you *do*. *Love*, the verb, means "to hold dear, cherish; desire, take pleasure in; to feel affection."

It's *love*, the verb, that most people have a problem with. Those three words—"I love you"—fall off the lips of lovers in heat like beads of sweat in the desert. When asked to demonstrate that love, some of those same lovers fall short. Love is work. Many of the people who pass through our lives are unwilling to make the commitment or sacrifices necessary for love to work. And frankly, sometimes, we don't either.

Love is elusive and unpredictable. Some people think love can be bought or sold, so they treat you to a movie or dinner and expect you to hand over your heart, soul, and body within twenty-four hours. And Cupid doesn't help. This little character prowls around, day and night, looking for potential lovers. But he doesn't always do a very good job of screening them, so he makes a lot of mistakes.

We can't blame Cupid, though. After all, his job description clearly states "to create opportunities for people to meet and fall in love"—not *stay* in love. If we're going to give some mystical, magical creature named Cupid—who says love is blind—the power to choose our mate, then once again, we deserve what we get. We are so afraid of that great void in our life and the question of who will fill it, that when we are "unmanned" we mistake a pretty smile and two phone calls in one day as love.

Love is addictive, a fact that keeps even the sanest of us in and out of affairs, looking for love in all the wrong places, trying to satisfy that addiction. We don't want to be alone, so it doesn't matter that we're not traveling the same path as a potential partner is. It doesn't matter that he's shallow, preoccupied with self, or too obsessed with his own fragile ego to return our love. Or that we were ten times happier alone than we are when we are with him. It doesn't even matter that the only thing we have in common is the desire to make *him* happy! We've convinced ourselves that nothing else matters. We've simply got to be in love.

We don't dream of just being in love, though. We're not looking for a relationship. We want *the* relationship! The real thing. We want to date only a "marriageable" guy, just in case he decides that he's ready to get married. And we know the rules. If he's not ready, it's not going to happen. Or, if it happens and he's not ready, it's not going to last. Unfortunately, with the shortage of available or desirable men, dating only marriageables may not always be possible. In fact, it may be next to impossible.

The pool of available, desirable men—particularly African American men—is shrinking dramatically. We're losing generations of beautiful Black boys and men to drugs and alcohol, AIDS, violence, illiteracy, suicide, and hopelessness. Others are choosing a homosexual life style. In the end, fewer of the desirable ones seem to be getting married these days and when they do, they're getting married later in life, choosing younger women or women of other ethnic groups. Many of them take advantage of the male-female imbalance in our community. More than one brother has point-blank told me that he's not in a hurry to get married because he feels obligated to do his share of "comforting" those of us who just can't seem to do without him (don't make me gag!).

Sounds kind of bleak for single Black women, doesn't it? Not really. Depends on how you look at it, and who's doing the looking. If you are an unmarried woman who has refused to accept the fact that some of us are simply not going to get married—no matter how attractive, how intelligent, how educated, how connected we are—then it will look bleak. Put your life on hold and abdicate responsibility for creating your own happiness, now, today—which is all any of us has—and it will look pretty dark right now.

Obsess with being "coupled" rather than celebrating your wholeness as a single woman, and it probably looks real gloomy right about now. If you're unattached and happen to be going through life solo at the moment, do yourself a favor! Take a break from your pity party for a few minutes and let's examine what it is that we think we're missing by not being involved in a relationship:

Stage #1—This is the initial stage in dating, and the password is *attraction.* You meet someone, your heart starts beating fast every time you're around him, and you decide that you like him. A few days or weeks or months later (depending on how fast you work or how afraid you are he'll move on), you decide to "do it." This initial stage is usually primal. Your animal instincts take over. You're attracted by what you see and smell. This is where women get in trouble because in most instances, women give their hearts first and then their bodies. Men, on the other hand, prefer to share their bodies first and then their hearts. (I'm generalizing again but there is a lot of truth in what I'm saying, so get over it!)

Sex for love or love for sex is nothing new. Human beings have been doing it for thousands of years. Women usually need a reason to have sex with a complete stranger. The promise of undying love or a "real" relationship sounds like pretty good reasons to some of us, so we do it. If we have what we consider "decent" reasons to sleep with someone, then we think we won't feel cheap or used or guilty if he never calls again. Sometimes this works and sometimes it doesn't.

On the other hand, thousands of women who do not have a steady man in their lives have made the adjustment to the shortage of desirable men by choosing to have sex without a good reason other than that they want to. Unlike some of us, these women are comfortable with their sexuality. They know what they want and they go after it. They have sex (safe sex, I hope) on a regular basis with men (single men, I hope) that they care about, but they have no delusions about being in a long-term relationship. They've taken charge of their lives and their bodies and dare anyone to condemn them for doing so.

However, for a great majority of women, sex for sex's sake doesn't work. Although a lot of them may also be comfortable with their sexuality, they have chosen not to allow their physical needs to dictate their lives. They know how dangerous it is to sleep with anybody and everybody today. The intimacy of sex without the intimacy of a relationship just doesn't work for them. They are holding out for open, loving, honest, monogamous relationships. Many of them have chosen celibacy (long- or short-term) rather than settling for booty calls. What they are looking for, along with a few good men, is a few good reasons!

Stage #2—I call the next stage limited dating. At this stage, you can forget about going to a club where he takes the risk of running into some of his buddies who might assume he has a "regular" woman now. Truth be told, the foundation of this relationship is usually still based on sex, but the fringe benefits— flowers, dinner, movies—are pleasant frills, so we so-called good girls don't necessarily feel guilty the morning after. Some relationships never make it past stage two. Those of us with stars in our eyes still see some possibilities in this stage, but deep down in our spirit we know he's not Mr. Right. We justify it by saying that at least we're not sitting around yearning for Mr. Right.

It's an open relationship. You may suspect that you are not the only woman in his life but you can live without the gory details. You simply let everything flow. The sex is decent, you enjoy each other, and your self-esteem is left intact because you feel you have a few good reasons to be there. Limited dating can include ex-boyfriends, ex-husbands (if you can stand them), long-distance romances, men who can't commit, and sometimes, unfortunately, married men (more about these beasts later). The password in Stage #2 is *availability*.

Stage #3—simply stated, is what most of us yearn for—a relationship. A combination of more frequent contact, steady dates, more intimate and in-depth conversations. The sex gets better, and your man actually doesn't mind introducing you to a few of his friends (his mother may still be off-limits in this stage). The flip side, of course, is that there are more disagreements or lovers' spats: Everyone knows that the more you see of each other, the more you can become your real self. The more your real self comes in contact with the other person's real self, the more flaws you're both going to see. The more flaws you see, the more you wonder what you saw in each other in the first place.

However, the good things seem to outweigh the bad, so you're willing to compromise and try to work out the kinks. Some women refer to this stage as a "good relationship" because there is some degree of commitment to our partner and to the relationship. Whatever we choose to call it, at this stage you get more of everything because both of you are not afraid to give more. The password in Stage #3, therefore, should be obvious: It's *more*!

Stage #4—The next stage is the ultimate, the champagne of relationships, the cream of the crop. It's not just *a* relationship. It's an exclusive relationship. Me for you and you for me.

At this stage, there is usually less traditional dating—less getting dressed up and going out—because, frankly, the chase is over (although some of us wish that people would put as much energy into the relationship as they put into the chase). You spend more time together, sharing each other's space and dreams. You plan vacations together. You may even exchange keys and meet his mother. The subject of marriage may suddenly escape from his lips without warning. And, mysteriously, the two of you actually start making long-range plans (translation: anything past the weekend).

You're pretty content. You may even be in love. You've finally connected with someone. There is a degree of consistency in what he does and what he says. You don't feel as though you've given up your independence or given your love to the wrong person. You're building something for the future. You feel this is about as close to heaven as you're going to get here on earth. The password at this stage is *commitment*.

Stage #5—The final stage in the male-female relationship (this side of divorce, of course) is marriage. Your wildest dreams have come true! You've found someone who can be monogamous for more than one night, so you've given yourself permission to trust completely for the first time in a long time. Marriage: the ultimate in love, sex, bad breath, and ring-around-the-collar. What more could we ask for? Isn't this what we've been pining for? Dreaming about? The password at Stage #5 is *love* (with a generous dose of luck).

So we're back where we started. Trying to get to Stage #5 without becoming obsessed with it. Looking to love and to be loved. Did we ever figure out what love is? I would not be so egotistical as to define it for you, but for me . . .

Love is having someone you can count on.

Love is romance and passion. Loyalty and trust.

Love is commitment and consistency. Respect and responsibility.

Love is friendship and fidelity. Affection and humor. Patience and tolerance.

Love is two grown people acting like they can't do without each other (until they find someone else).

Love is that chance at happiness that some of us won't take time to find within ourselves.

Girlfriend, love is truly a trip! Long live love!

8

Bad Boy Alert: Just Say No!

"If the cake is bad, what good is the frosting?"

O nce you've fallen out of love or been dumped on or had your heart broken once or twice, it's easy to say that you're not going to let it happen again. You start making promises to yourself: I'm not going to date anyone who isn't ready for a real relationship! I'm not going to let anyone in my life ever again unless he's ready to make a commitment! I'm definitely not going to take any more crap!

It's only fair that we become more selective about the men we become involved with and learn to make better and more conscious decisions since we ultimately are the ones who have to live with those decisions. Unfortunately, we have short memories when we meet someone who turns us on. The brain takes a coffee break. The heart beats overtime and frequently speaks louder than logic or common sense. All of a sudden it doesn't matter if you have absolutely nothing in common with each other or that he picks his nose in public or that he hasn't had a steady job since he was sixteen. All of a sudden, all that matters is that you like him and he likes you.

However, whether we like it or not, there are some men that women should avoid like the plague. Don't let loneliness be a reason to renege on this rule: Stay away from men who may be available (accessible) but are simply not "acceptable." Don't, under any circumstances, allow them on to your list.

What's acceptable? Only you can answer that. *Webster's* defines *acceptable* as "worth receiving." So only you can decide if a man meets this criteria. It's up to you to determine that he's worth taking up time and space in your life. You and you alone choose what's important to you in a relationship. If you've set boundaries, only you know what you're willing to tolerate. When you decide that you will not tolerate deceit or profanity or drugs, then you must be strong enough to stand by those decisions even when you meet someone who makes your heart go pitter-patter.

One of the most important lessons I've learned in life is that the more you love and respect yourself, the less you're willing to tolerate. I have realized that the more you are willing to put up with, the more bad behavior becomes the norm. Once you start shifting your boundaries to allow a man into your life with a drinking problem, the next thing you know, you have decided drugs are okay once in a while. Physical abuse suddenly becomes the norm after you've allowed yourself to be slapped once or twice. Allow someone to stand you up three times in a row without a legitimate reason, and it'll soon be easier for him to disrespect you in other ways. It becomes increasingly difficult to separate what's acceptable behavior and what's unacceptable behavior. The boundary lines become blurred and the next thing you know, you're in cahoots with an undesirable.

If the bad times are outweighing the good and you're sorry

you ever met this man, then you're probably involved with an undesirable. If looking in the mirror the morning after is a traumatic experience, you've probably spent the night with an undesirable. Sharing your bed, your heart, and the most intimate secrets of your body and soul with an undesirable who still looks undesirable in the morning (bad breath and all) is masochistic. If you find yourself with an undesirable against your better judgment, even if you think you love yourself, feelings of self-contempt and self-hatred can creep up, whisper in your ear, and make you feel like a loser.

The secret is to provide yourself enough love and warmth and kindness and understanding and positive reinforcement that even when huge black clouds follow you around for days or weeks after an encounter with an undesirable, you can still be confident that the clouds will pass, the sun will shine again, and you will survive.

The secret is to remember that you are the producer, director, and star of your own life. It is your drama (or comedy) and your ultimate goal should be to survive (and thrive) without an endless army of undesirable men moving in and out of your life. And speaking of armies, think of your life as a battleground. It's the good guys versus the bad guys. Good choices versus bad choices. Since you're the commander in chief, you get to choose. It's your life and it's the only one you've got, so you shouldn't be afraid to make firm, tough decisions.

This take-charge attitude may be difficult to adjust to in the beginning, particularly if you're a card-carrying masochist as so many women are (the truth hurts, doesn't it?). Some of us are so used to going through life allowing other people to define us and decide for us and choose for us that we have difficulty taking charge of our life. If we want to be happy and fulfilled, we've got to answer some very important questions that only we can know the answers to: What do I really want? What don't I want? Where am I willing to compromise?

Curiously enough, most of us usually can't describe what we really want out of life. But we'll tell you in a New York minute what we don't want. Most of us know, for example, that just because a man is available doesn't mean he's acceptable as a potential mate. We know this, and yet our actions (getting involved anyway) contradict it. If you're one of the few million women who are having difficulty distinguishing between men who are simply *available* and those who are *acceptable*, I've compiled a reference list for you.

There are men who should be automatically eliminated from your list of real prospects if you are seriously interested in beginning and/or maintaining a healthy, meaningful, long-term relationship. They include:

1. Homosexuals: Gay men can make wonderful friends, but that's where the relationship should end. To try to find romance with a man who is not interested in being intimate with a woman is just looking for heartache.

The exception is, of course, the very sensitive, clean-cut, earring-wearing sweetie who is going through an identity crisis and trying to pass as heterosexual. If you are one of the unfortunate sisters who finds out that you have unwittingly fallen in love with a gay man who is trying to convince himself he is straight, please don't blame yourself. Your sexuality is not in question; he is struggling to come to terms with his. Reflect on the positive moments in the relationship, thank God you found out before you begged him to do the nasty and move on. Remind yourself that everything that looks good *to* you is not good *for* you! Be grateful that your antennae go up when you meet someone who prefers men over women. It's not your job to spend the next ten years of your life trying to change him into something he can't be—a heterosexual.

2. Bisexuals: What you really have to worry about is guys who say they are straight but actually go both ways. These guys are hard to recognize and it's even harder to protect yourself—all I can say is trust your instincts and practice safe sex always!

3. Asexuals: Unless you don't care about sex, you may want to stay clear of these guys. For whatever reasons, they won't (or can't) have sex. This is not a bad thing if sex is not somewhere on your list of druthers. But if sex *is* on your list and you get a little excited one night, all these sweethearts can do is throw you in a cold shower. You've been warned!

4. Drug addicts (and pushers): Anyone who doesn't give a damn about himself or those kids he sells drugs to, obviously doesn't deserve me. It's just that simple. In fact, I wish some of us would use some of the energy we spend worrying about being single and help get some of these dope fiends off the streets. All the rhetoric in the world could not possibly convince me that a drug addict loved me; how could he, when he unmistakably does not love himself? When he gets desperate for a fix, he would probably trade you for five dollars' worth of crack any day. Do your Christian duty: Refer him to a treatment facility—but keep your heart (and pocketbook) as far away from him as humanly possible. Drug addicts and pushers are too selfish and have too little regard for human life for us to consider them desirable.

5. Alcoholics: If you fall in love with an alcoholic, get ready for expensive liquor bills. Don't be surprised if you also experience wet toilet seats, some violence, and some impotence—even when he's sober. Although alcoholism is considered a disease—and I sympathize with anyone who has a disease—I am not professionally trained to help someone kick such a serious habit. Although we may enjoy impersonating Florence Nightingale now and then, few of us are qualified to give an alcoholic the kind of treatment and support he so desperately needs. Often when we meet someone with a drinking problem, we quickly forget that there is little we can do for him if he won't help himself. We inevitably believe that we can get to the root of his problem. So we hide the booze, drive him to AA meetings three times a week, and think we'll live happily and soberly ever after. The truth is:

(a) Unless he wants to stop drinking, he never will.
(b) Your love (and nagging and tears and threats) may not be enough to encourage him to stop.
(c) You'll probably suffer as much as (or more than) he does during his binges.

I'm not suggesting that women should completely write off this potential hope chest of available men. Like most African American women, I'm aware of the devastating effect of substance abuse on our friends and loved ones. Just proceed with caution. If you miss the obvious (and sometimes not-so-obvious) signs of this chronic, debilitating disease and inadvertently fall in love with an alcoholic, try to convince him to get professional help. But if you can't and he won't, don't blame yourself. Don't stop loving yourself, because you'll need a lover around more than ever. And that lover may be you.

6. Verbal or physical abusers A.K.A. all-around bastards: In one brief sentence, leave these crazies alone! Occasionally, some of us unwittingly get involved with men who must show their superiority by kicking ass, preferably ours. Just for the record, this is totally unacceptable behavior for women who love themselves. If you allow such a madman to take his fears and insecurities out on you, you will be giving him the power to control your body and life that are rightfully yours.

We simply can't spend a lifetime patching ourselves back up time and time again and making excuses for our man's temper tantrums. A healthy relationship depends on the maturity and emotional well-being of each partner. How can anyone who professes to love you break your arms and give you black eyes? Apparently, somebody doesn't know the meaning of love. Unless you're into kinky sex, love should not be painful.

If he insists on nurturing his destructive behavior or reverting to adolescent scenes like having fits and kicking your behind because it makes him feel good about himself, or if he is unable (or unwilling) to meet the challenges of being a grown-up in a grown-up world, where real men have to take responsibility for their actions, your decision to leave him should be a relatively easy one. It boils down to him or you. Your sanity or his. Your life or his. Get rid of the SOB as quickly as you can and thank God you had the courage to do it before he killed you. (Anyway, everyone knows that men who beat women are usually wimps with bad breath and little bitty things!)

7. Cannibals: These irresponsible, immature, insecure, insensitive hound dogs are usually out to prove that they can get it up with anybody anytime. They are so preoccupied with self-gratification that they don't care who gets hurt. These men really need more than sex to make them true men but they are too stupid (and irresponsible and immature and insecure and insensitive) to realize it. These men usually treat women the way cannibals treat flesh. They chew it up and if they like it, they swallow it. If they don't, they spit it out. Similarly, these men leave a mess wherever they go, particularly in the lives of the unknowing women who meet these twentieth-century cannibals who urinate and think with the same organ.

If you give the cannibal a 325 BMW, a Tommy shirt, a pair of Nikes, a pleather (plastic and leather) briefcase, and a slightly exaggerated penis, he thinks he's God's gift to the opposite sex! But even sadder than the cannibal's profile is that a lot of women who recognize his modus operandi decide that they can change him or help him "find" himself anyway. The fact is that he's lost and he doesn't know that he's lost, so he's not looking for himself. So why in heaven do we think *we* can find him? He might find himself one day—but only if he admits he's lost his way. He can't change until he wants to.

Like most cannibals, he probably won't admit that he has a problem. How can he solve it if he won't admit it? If we keep nagging him about changing, he'll eventually start to blame us for being the way he is. After all, he doesn't have a problem. It's our problem. Why? Because we won't accept him the way he is. He's no different than he was when we met him. He was a cannibal then and he's a cannibal now. And you know what? He'll be right. It is our problem. Nothing's changed. He's the same man we went gaga over at the beginning. Either we'll have to accept him or move on. Without a real commitment to change, the cannibal won't.

To be fair, not all of these men were born cannibals. Many of them are kind and sensitive lovers and friends who unfortunately are haunted by memories of bad childhoods, dysfunctional families, vindictive ex-wives, doggish ex-girlfriends, rejection, low self-esteem, pursue-conquer-assassinate mentalities, you name it. So what happens? These former good guys end up dumping on you. Dumping all their anger and frustrations and guilt on you because you happen to be there. Immaturity and insecurity seem to be a requirement for this boy-man. He can be between twenty-five and sixty-five years old but chronically behaves like a thirteen year old when he's around you. He's selfish, greedy, and self-centered. He's attempting to get back at everybody who ever "done him wrong" by doing you wrong.

Most cannibals are just afraid. Why should they be afraid, you ask? Men run the world. They make most of the decisions. They call most of the shots. What are they afraid of? A lot of men are simply afraid of being afraid. They're afraid of fear. Fear has become their number one enemy. They're afraid of loving but more afraid of not being loved. They're afraid of intimacy, but more afraid of being alone. They're afraid of sex without love and love without sex.

Wait! you say. *That last statement can't be true! Did you say men are afraid of love without sex and sex without love?* You damn tootin'! I certainly did! Sure, a lot of cannibals ultimately are there for just the sex but at the same time, their egos have to be stroked. That means that they want you to care enough about them to make the ultimate sacrifice (next to having their baby), and that's dropping your pants. They want to feel that you don't do it with just anybody or everybody. They want to feel special (who doesn't?). When they've conned you into having a physical relationship without making a commitment, that makes them feel special. Bottom line, even the cannibal wants to feel special. Even he needs more than just sex, even though he hasn't realized it yet.

Don't *you* be stupid! Unless you're a trained psychologist or want to throw away a few years of your life trying to fix him, it's not your job to show him the way home. Your job is to keep stepping before you get chewed up and spit out like a piece of bad liver.

8. The walking wounded: Usually these are men who have been divorced for less than two years and didn't have a choice in the matter. Sometimes, they are men whose wives played around on them (good luck trying to get one of them to admit this). The walking wounded are usually very bitter and it may be difficult for you to understand why at the beginning. Sometimes it's because he really wanted the marriage to work. Sometimes it's because he didn't get to file first. Sometimes it's because he feels he got screwed in court. Sometimes it's because his ego can never forgive his ex-wife's affairs. So if we fall in love with him, you and I have to pay for her indiscretions for the remainder of our natural lives.

If you choose to date one of the walking wounded in spite of my warning, wear heavy armor to protect yourself, especially around your heart. Women usually find it relatively easy to love the walking wounded because they appear to be so vulnerable, lonely, and despondent. The walking wounded usually reach out to anyone who is reasonably nice and will listen to them refer to their ex-wife as "my wife" ten or twelve times during the length of your first, second, or even third date. After a while, no matter how much you may care about this man, you will find yourself having to suppress the urge to tell him to shut up when he starts talking about his ex-wife—particularly if you're in the middle of a romantic evening for two, not three.

Although the walking wounded have a desperate need for companionship, until they have fully recovered they are usually unprepared for the big C—commitment. Some of them can't even say the word without stuttering. Many of them are angry, shell-shocked, weaving in and out of moodiness through an invisible revolving door. The first woman who comes into their life will have a thankless job: that of tolerating his pain and grief until he recovers—if he ever does.

If you recognize the symptoms of the walking wounded going into a relationship and you can be patient, you may have found yourself a good lover and a wonderful friend. He will be grateful for your patience and you'll feel good thinking about what you've helped create. You should know, however, that oftentimes—after you've hung in and he's recovered—he'll resume the search for the real Ms. Right. You may have been a pit stop or temporary refuge, so be prepared to lose both a lover and a friend.

Be careful, however, not to fall in love with too many of the walking wounded in your lifetime. Even though they're a little confused at the beginning (*crazy* may be a better word), some of them are really good guys, with many of the traits that you've been looking for in the man of your dreams. If he is one of the good guys, be prepared: It might take a long time to get him out of your system. When someone you care about is constantly searching for someone to love besides *you*, it could be hazardous to your health. If you love yourself and believe that you have a right to be happy, you simply can't afford to be in love with someone who's not in love with you. Again, thank God that you can see clearly and move on before you get your walking papers. Case closed.

9. The chronically unemployed: Because of the high rate of unemployment in the African American community, automatically eliminating the chronically unemployed from our list of desirables may upset a few people. They may accuse me of being insensitive to the needs of unskilled and underskilled brothers who really do want to work but who, for various reasons—some beyond their control—have been unable to find suitable employment. How do you tell the difference between a brother who's worked for fifteen years and was laid off when the company downsized from the brother who hasn't looked for a job in fifteen years?

Easy. Impersonate Sherlock Holmes. Ask questions. Give

him a lie detector if you have to. Listen to his rap and see where his head is. Take off the rose-colored glasses and open your eyes. It shouldn't be difficult to identify Mr. Do Nothing, Mr. Be Nothing, and Mr. Have Nothing. He'll be doing nothing, being nothing, and having nothing. If you can accept his lack of ambition or desire to be gainfully employed, then so be it. If it doesn't bother you that your man doesn't get up, get dressed, and go to work every morning, more power to you.

But let's think about this for a minute. If your man chooses to remain unemployed and it doesn't bother you at least a little bit, it might be time for some self-examination. Why *don't* you care that he doesn't get up and go to work? Why *doesn't* it matter that he lies in bed all day and watches *The Young and the Restless, All My Children*, and *Guiding Light*? Why doesn't it bother you that he doesn't bring home some of the bacon some of the time?

Studies have shown that, for better or worse, a man's self-esteem and self-worth are inextricably tied into what he does for a living. If this is true, it may be somewhat difficult (though not impossible) for a man who chooses to be chronically unemployed to have high self-esteem. So why aren't his self-esteem and self-worth important to you? Why are you in love with (and willing to financially support) a man who does not see the value of meaningful employment? If you ask yourself these questions, it may occur to you that *you* may have the problem. His choice not to work and your choice to accept his chronic unemployment makes two statements—one about him and one about you. Don't get mad—just think about it!

10. Criminals (active and retired): First, if they're really actively engaged in criminal activity, pray that the cops arrest them before you become too involved with them. We all know that a disproportionate number of African American men are in jails and prisons all across the nation. We also know that many of them are there because of a history of racism and prejudice in the American legal system. But lest we forget and assume that all the brothers in prison are innocent, remember what comedian Richard Pryor said after visiting one of our state institutions: *"Thank God we got prisons!"*

If you ever become desperately lonely and think of turning to prisons for a pen pal, keep in mind these three facts:

(a) Long-distance love is usually no love at all, especially if he's serving a life sentence behind bars;

(b) if he's not serving a life sentence or on death row, your Al Capone Jackson may get out one day; and

(c) if and when lover boy gets out, you'd better pray that he *really was* innocent!

Now this doesn't mean you should desert your lover just because he was arrested. He really could be innocent! Maybe he didn't steal that new thirty-two-inch television in your living room from the little old lady around the corner. Just because he didn't have any money when he left last night and he didn't bring the TV home until 4 A.M. and the police photo looks a little like him, it could still be a case of mistaken identity. Regardless, once he has been arrested, convicted, and sent away to the slammer, you have to determine if you are willing to make the sacrifices necessary to be a gangster's moll after he gets out. Are you ready for the police stakeouts and the possibility of stolen property by the ton filling up your garage? Only you can decide.

Once you decide to get (or stay) involved with an ex-convict (they prefer to be called former inmates), follow your instincts. It shouldn't be too difficult to decide if the love of your life plans to walk a straight line after he gets out of prison. If he has learned his lesson and decides prison is not for him, he may be a perfect mate for you. He'll appreciate his freedom and probably do anything within the law to protect it.

On the other hand, if the man you love gives you subtle hints that he doesn't plan to mend his ways (hints like keeping an arsenal of automatic weapons, wearing a mask to work, or sleep-walking in banks at 3 A.M.), you might want to reconsider your decision to give him another chance. At some point, you become an accessory to his criminal acts, particularly if he's bringing the goodies home to you. Don't ever be afraid or ashamed to say that you made a mistake or that you've changed your mind about the relationship. Better late than never. If you feel threatened and are afraid to break it off, talk to a friend or a family member. Talk to your minister. Find a shelter. Just get away. If he seems too hot to handle, he probably is. Drop him like a hot potato and get on with your crime-free life. You deserve better!

11. Black men with "vanilla fever": These are men preoccupied with White women, the forbidden fruit. Men who are looking for their identity in the White man's bed and need a constant reminder of the Mandingo myth. For years, Black women have tried to ignore Black men with vanilla fever. After all, they represent only 1 percent of the Black men in this country. But it's been a very difficult pill to swallow, particularly for baby boomers, whose pool of desirable men shrank dramatically between the late '60s and early '70s, when we lost thousands of decent Black men to the trauma and slaughter of the Vietnam War. Then in the late '70s and well into the '80s, we started losing thousands of our men to illegal drugs and violence. The late '80s and the '90s have brought two more epidemics: AIDS and crack. To add insult to injury, in the midst of all this carnage, we started losing high-profile brothers—successful athletes, entertainers, politicians—to White women.

Unfortunately, some of us can't handle even one brother "coloring" outside the lines, even though we have noticed an increase in Black women dating White men. We either stare in disgust at interracial couples or try to pretend we don't see them standing in front of us in line at the grocery store or the movies. We get angrier still if the brother is good-looking and she's a dog. We really go ballistic if he's successful and has the financial means to treat her like a queen. Many of us begin to question our own self-worth, our own femininity, and even start to believe the Black-women-castrate-their-men myth.

Well, in a word—*don't*! Don't stare! Don't loud-talk them! Don't call them names! Don't make a fool of yourself. And for God's sake, don't get angry! His decision to date a White woman has absolutely nothing to do with you personally. Please don't walk through your one solitary life nursing your resentment or hatred of the Black/White thing. This racist attitude can be a real handicap in your attempt to find personal satisfaction, happiness, and fulfillment in your own life. Truth be told, girlfriend, it's really none of your business!

If the Black male/White female union is one of the demons that drives your blood pressure up—particularly when it's in your face in a magazine, on television, or in public—tell that demon to get lost. A negative attitude about something over which you have no control is very destructive. Take some of that energy you spend trying to take care of his business and his life and invest it in your own business and your own life.

There are far too many undesirables to mention all of them. If I tried to, I'd never finish the rest of the book! But if you need a few more examples, don't be afraid to reach back, dredge up a few undesirables from your own files, thank God you didn't marry them, and then move on!

As a matter of fact, it's time to move on past the undesirables anyway, to the good guys . . . the genuine brothers . . . the real men!

9

Meeting Real Men

"You meet a lot of guys but very few men."

Contrary to popular belief, all women do not believe that all men are bad (or bad for us). We know there are some good guys out there. Some real men. We've seen them from a distance. We've talked to them or know someone who has. We have friends who brag about being married to them. Unfortunately, we've met enough of the bad ones to know that they're out there too. But hope springs eternal. We haven't given up. Most of us still trust that someone, somewhere has our name written on his heart.

We want to believe that the undesirable men we meet are not a reflection of the whole gender. But as the days and months and years pass, it becomes more of a challenge. Every time we meet someone who is unable or unwilling to commit to the kind of relationship that we think we deserve, we become even more cautious about dancing with wolves again. Unfortunately, the more we strike out, the less we trust our instincts.

We forget that there are tremendous possibilities for growth and change, even in relationships that don't work. Relationships that don't work are not all bad. Some relationships are meant to be but not meant to last. The ones that don't last can make us wiser and stronger. They offer us great opportunities to become focused on the kind of man we really want in our life. Once we've had our share of undesirables, it should become easier to decide what we want and don't want. Unfortunately, even after we've decided, we sometimes lose our focus. You meet a good-looking, smooth-talking hunk who gives your ego a quick fix, and the next thing you know, you're involved again with someone who you know is not right for you, someone who is on his way to breaking your heart and scattering the pieces all over your bedroom.

If we are serious about breaking the cycle of getting involved in bad relationships, we can't afford the luxury of moving the boundaries of common sense every other day just to accommodate our loneliness and self-pity because we've spent another Friday night alone. We need to stand firm and keep our eyes on the prize. If that prize is a "real man," then we've got to hold out for him.

Holding out isn't easy. Especially if you don't have any interests beyond finding a man. Holding out won't be easy if you've resigned yourself to the role of victim in your own life and don't have the courage to make an interesting life for yourself. Holding out isn't easy if your friends and family and coworkers all insist that you're being too choosy. But most of all, holding out won't be easy if you don't believe you have a right to be with someone special.

If you're tired of saving up and giving all your love to the wrong person, holding out might not be so hard. If you're tired of the one-night encounters with strangers who never call again, if you're tired of settling for less than your heart desires, holding out shouldn't be a chore. If you're tired of the lies and deceit and pain and disappointments, holding out won't be that hard. If you've made up your mind that you deserve more because you have so much more to give, that it's more courageous to be alone than to wake up with someone you wish wasn't there, then holding out will get easier.

We can't wait for our men to change. They may never change. *We* have to change. We have to change our attitudes, our expectations. If the men in our lives don't want the same thing we want from a relationship, we must exercise our right to choose. This can mean having the courage to give up and walk away if he's unwilling or unable to make changes or compromises that will improve the relationship. If we're unhappy and choose to stay, then we must stay on his terms. Keep in mind that under his terms, he doesn't have an obligation to change. If you choose to stay and he never changes, you are not the victim. There is no victim here, so stop impersonating one. You've chosen to stay, so you get what you deserve.

Holding out doesn't mean having unrealistic expectations about love and life. Life is hard work. Love is hard work. If you don't believe this, maybe your expectations are too high for what you have to offer. Maybe you need to check yourself out. You want a real man? Maybe your real man wants a real woman. Are you loving and giving? Are you willing to compromise and make changes for the good of the relationship? Are you willing to do what it takes to become the kind of person that he needs? Are you a real woman in search of a real man?

While we are on the subject, what is a real man? Is there such a thing as a real man? How can we tell the difference between a real man and an undesirable one? What separates the real men from the men who take pleasure in breaking our hearts into little pieces? Do real men really exist? I thought you'd never ask.

A real man is sensitive, caring, gentle, thoughtful, and respectful, not necessarily in that order and not necessarily all the time, but at least he tries. A real man remembers birthdays, anniversaries, and holidays. He loves to make you happy, because it makes him happy. He's familiar with the telephone and knows what to do with it when he's going to be late. He helps his woman do their housework. He doesn't care if his buddies see him cooking or doing laundry because he is his own man and has nothing to prove. A real man admits that he knows nothing about repairing the microwave, the lawn mower, or the car. He doesn't think twice about calling an electrician, a gardener, or a mechanic instead of trying to do it himself and blowing up the house or the car.

A real man is secure enough to understand that a plane needs copilots; that a winning team usually has more than one coach. He doesn't always have to be the quarterback or carry the ball. He is willing to share some of the power in the game. He knows you well enough to know that you are smart enough to do more than stand on the sidelines and be a cheerleader. His manhood is not threatened when you use the brain God gave you. He not only admires you for making decisions in the partnership but respects your right to do so.

A real man doesn't leave dirty socks and stiff shorts on the floor next to the hamper in the bathroom expecting his fairy godmother to levitate by and pick them up. A real man appreciates the toilet seat, since he has to occasionally use it himself; he doesn't get angry when he has to put it in its proper place for the woman he loves.

Real men still open and close doors to cars and buildings. They do so not because they have to but because they want to. They don't believe all that nonsense about women not wanting them to open doors, light cigarettes, or send flowers (undesirables probably started those ridiculous rumors!).

A real man is not afraid to say no or hear no, so he doesn't have to take what he wants. Women will give it to him. He's not afraid to apologize or say, "I'm sorry." He knows that admitting a mistake makes him an even bigger man. Real men seldom lie but even when they do, people they love usually don't get hurt.

A real man does not forsake his woman for his male friends or hide his woman from his female friends. If he goes out with the boys, he doesn't have to rap to the girls to prove anything to his boys.

A real man does not get physical anywhere except in the gym or on the basketball court. He believes that only raccoons should ever have black eyes and that only trees should ever have broken limbs.

A real man is never an atheist. He believes in God. He does not believe that the earth and everything that is in the earth and under the earth and above the earth "just happened." He's not afraid to express his love for God in a church pew, a factory, or a football stadium. He believes that we are our brother's keeper and that we all have a responsibility to one another.

A real man loves Black women! After all, his mother and sisters and aunts and grandmothers are all Black women. He respects Black women for who they are and what they've meant to our survival here, on foreign soil, far away from the motherland. He's not so eager to go tiptoeing around in someone else's backyard trying to find out where he belongs. A real man knows that he belongs here at home, with us.

A real man understands that *monogamy* means "one woman at a time." Everything on the menu may be tempting, but grown people have to choose. If he doesn't want to be here anymore, he should leave—not sneak around until he gets caught or catches something and gives it to you.

A real man has a dream in his heart. He is ambitious and appreciates a good job, a good car, and a good home. But he understands that all of these material things cannot replace a good woman, a good lover, a good friend. A real man chooses to be a loving, responsible husband, father, lover, and friend.

A real man knows that most women love romance and even if he is not romantic by nature, he knows that an unexpected hug or kiss (without pawing and groping) is always appreciated and usually well rewarded.

A real man gives abundantly because he expects to receive abundantly. He knows that sex without love is just so-so, but that sex with someone you love is the ultimate aphrodisiac. When a real man loves a woman, he takes the time to find out what satisfies her. He cares if she gets hers before he gets his and he knows that in most instances—including sex—haste makes waste.

A real man is confident. He needs his space, so he is not afraid to give space to people he cares about. He is not afraid to say, "I love you" or "I need you" to someone he loves and needs. He knows that love comes from the soul and not from the lips.

A real man has a conscience and knows the pain of a lie and the power of the truth.

A real man is a friend and lover to his friend and lover.

A real man—in a nutshell—is not afraid of a real woman!

Where, you ask in anticipation, do you meet real men? Where do you think? *Anywhere you can!* Anywhere you might be. Widen your peripheral vision. Remember, while you are looking for someone, someone may be looking for you. Stop putting men in boxes because of the way they look, how tall they are, how much hair they have (or don't have), where they work or live, how much money they have (or don't have). Stop writing off potentially good, decent men because you place more value on his height than on his heart. Stop putting value on superficial things that have nothing to do with building a foundation for a relationship.

Someone once said, "Greener pastures often have higher fences around them." That means we can't always expect real men to fall into our lap. We may need to extend ourselves beyond the barriers that we've put up to protect ourselves. We may need to smile more and stop frowning when a brother speaks to us at a gas station, car wash, or supermarket. We may need to get outside our fences and take up a new hobby, visit an art gallery, or attend that New Year's Eve party that we've been avoiding the past few years.

If you're looking for a quiet, serious man, you're probably not going to find him on his feet, screaming at the referee at an athletic event. Skip the football games and spend some time at a library or museum. If you're looking for someone who's involved in his church, you're probably not going to find him in a bar every Friday night. Skip happy hour and get involved in a mission program or youth ministry at your church. Take a Bible study course at a church in another part of town. Enlarge your circle of female friends. They have brothers, uncles, friends, coworkers, all of whom open up new possibilities to meet someone special. But even if we don't meet Mr. Right through these efforts, we've taken charge of our life, had a little fun along the way, and made the moments of our life count.

So where do you meet real men? I repeat: Anywhere you can!

10

From Boys to Men

"There is no shame in not knowing, only in refusing to learn."

Our men must learn that they are human, with all of the frailties that come with being human. They must learn that they must give up their membership in the secret society that teaches them to be macho from birth to death, to hide their feelings and their tears. Why? Women (and by extension families and communities) are the ones who have to bear the burden of this Stone Age mentality. We are the ones who have to feed fiberglass egos so fragile that they shatter if we get them to admit that they care about us even a little bit. We are the ones who have to decipher what they really mean when they try to say what they can't say but wish they could.

Before they come to us with their arms open, looking for love and tenderness, they must be willing to show love and tenderness. We want men to enjoy our company as well as our body. We want them to learn to appreciate being held and touched and kissed without going all the way all the time. We want them to learn that when they're confused, we're confused. When they're in conflict, we're in conflict. When they hurt, we hurt. Our men must learn that it's okay to feel pain and sorrow and grief. It's okay to celebrate their youth but it's not okay to use their youth as an excuse to act like a child.

Our men must learn the meaning of honesty and then practice being honest with themselves and with us. Our men must learn that deceit hurts much more than the truth and that when they violate our trust, they are violating our spirit and our body. Our men must learn that, frankly, we're tired. We're tired of the inconsiderate, infantile behavior that we've learned to tolerate and become all too familiar with. Rather than cancel a date, they become the Invisible Man for weeks at a time. They usually follow up this behavior with vacant promises, unfulfilled vows to be faithful but slip back into the familiar role of rogue and lover boy as soon as our backs are turned. Then we, like love-starved kittens, allow this antisocial behavior of lies covering up lies to carve our hearts into tiny little pieces to be chewed up and spit out again and again rather than face the singles plague.

Our men must learn to stop wallowing in self-pity and playing the victim. America has abused, misused, and mistreated the sons of Africa. That is an undisputed fact. But they were not the only ones abused, misused, and mistreated. They were not the only ones exploited. Black women were exploited as well. Black women were also kidnapped and chained and raped and beaten and victimized. We share the same painful history and yet we (including 67 percent of us who are raising our children alone) choose to go on in spite of the pain, in spite of the broken promises and stolen dreams.

Some of us have learned that we cannot surrender to the pain. We have too much to lose. Our children have too much to lose. Our community has too much to lose. We realize that we cannot change the past. We can only change the present, by changing ourselves so that, in the future, we stop the vicious cycle of finding someone to blame for where we are and why we can't seem to get ahead. The truth is that some of us can't get ahead because we're too busy looking behind us.

Slavery was real. It happened. But too many of our brothers are stuck where they are because they feel that somebody should pay for what was done to Blacks during that period of our nation's history. Somebody *is* paying. This nation is paying for it in more ways than you think. The drugs, the crime, the poverty, and the fear and resentment between the races are all residuals of the forced bondage and mistreatment of an entire race of human beings. Slavery had consequences. Maybe somebody should pay. But we can't make them pay, so we're going to have to move on, past the pain—and past the blame—to the present.

Speaking of blame, our men might want to learn to stop blaming Black women for taking jobs in White America that rightfully belong to them (go figure!) and be grateful that we can get jobs and keep jobs that support their children—and them if necessary. If they think that Black women are stealing their jobs, they might want to consider staying in high school and going on to college or trade school so they learn how to do something other than complain. Armed with an education, a few skills, and a little ambition, they may be able to find someone (family, friends, community groups) who will trust them with a few dollars to open up their own business. That way, they won't have to depend on the "White man's job," and they can support themselves and the babies that they make.

Our men must learn to stop accusing us of being too materialistic. For the record, it's not a sin to like nice, new, pretty things. It's not a sin to want to move out of public housing or away from the hood. It's not a sin to refuse to live half-naked under a bridge eating a can of pork and beans with somebody we love. We don't want to throw our love away on someone who's not willing to work as hard as we do to get the things we both want. Some of us don't mind working. Our men must learn that those of us who work, work hard—and usually have to kiss a lot of butts for our material comforts. And after our men leave us brokenhearted, again, sometimes our little condo, the Mazda, and the diamond ring we bought for ourselves may be all we have left to comfort us.

Our men must learn how painful and unfulfilling it is to be in love with someone who cannot give us anything but his body. It is also risky to love someone who wants to give his body to anybody and everybody. Having multiple sexual partners is not only stupid but dangerous. They must learn not to allow their physical needs to dictate their lives. They must learn that the intimacy of sex without the intimacy of a relationship may work for them but it doesn't work for many of us. Most of us want men in our lives who bring more than just passion to the table. We need passion *and* promise. Passion gives us pleasure and promise gives us hope.

Finally, our men must learn that although racial equality is and has always been a top priority for Black America, Black women must also be concerned about women's rights. Black women have had to work too long and too hard for what happiness and success we enjoy today. We have paid our dues and earned the right to feel safe and secure in a disease-free, drug-free, and abuse-free relationship. Anyone, male or female, Black or White, who tries to keep us from becoming all that God intends us to be had better get out of the way! We love you, Black man! I can't say that enough. And we want to share our lives with you. If you won't allow us to share it with you—with dignity and respect and love—we have no other choice. Like it or not, we'll go it alone.

11

Lessons Worth Learning

"There is no such thing as a free lunch."

I won't deny it! Living solo can be a desperate existence if we give in to the loneliness. It can be filled with fear, anxiety, rejection, increased risk of getting AIDS, and single servings of tuna and Jell-O. But wouldn't it be criminal to allow the temporary insecurities that build up because of our singleness to make us lose sight of the fact that we have a God-given right to be happy—with or without a mate?

What then is the answer to our dilemma? Do we continue to look for Mr. Right, for love and passion and romance and respect and honesty? Do we wait patiently? Pray harder? Cry longer? Do we surrender to our physical selves and become loose women? Do we allow ourselves to become prey to all the insecure, egotistical, heartless men who find pleasure in using, abusing, and manipulating us to suit their needs? Just what the heck do we do?

First, there are some things we must accept. We must accept that the problem is bigger than you and me. Statistically speaking, there are simply more single women than single men living in America today—Black *and* White. Eliminate the undesirables, Uncle Toms, scary-curls, pimps, psychopaths, and sissies, what have you got left? Not a helluva lot! I know it takes a while to sink in. The romantic side of my somewhat undeveloped brain is still fighting the reality that there are simply not enough eligible Black men to go around. Period.

The unblemished and painful truth is that not all of us will get married. Don't get hysterical! I know the truth hurts, but there's more. Some of us may not even fall in love in our lifetime (remember that's a temporary state anyway). The truth of the matter is that waiting for the perfect man to come into our lives at the perfect time is a perfect waste of time. (I made that up. Clever, isn't it?)

This doesn't mean that we should completely give up on ever meeting Mr. Right, but our journey should be as enjoyable as the destination. Black women have a reservoir of love to give, yet we become stingy with our love when it comes to ourselves. We start to ration our love as if we don't have enough to go around. If you believe that you were born to love someone, start here and now. Start with you. Say it: *I love me!* That's right. I said it. Now you say it: *I love me!* Say it loud: *I love me!* Say it like you mean it: *I love me!* In spite of my flaws and imperfections, *I love me.* In spite of my mistakes, *I love me.* And I accept this sacred gift of life as a miracle. I accept my singleness as another stage in life, like wearing my first bra or driving a car.

We must learn to stop looking at every man we meet as a potential mate, someone who has all the ingredients to save us. We must learn to stop believing that we can change men. We can't. We can only change the way they treat us. We can only offer them enough love so that they want to change. And even then, our love may not be enough.

Men and women are often playing for different stakes. We talk to our men and treat them as if we know what makes them tick. We don't know what makes them tick. We may think we do, but we don't. They don't know what makes us tick either. Like us, most of them are wearing masks to hide the anger, the hurt, the disappointment, the disillusionment with ourselves, each other, and life. We usually end up blaming everything from racism to misplaced values, but ultimately the solutions to our problems lie a lot closer to home—within ourselves.

It's easy to criticize the system that we think created these men we don't understand. Time after time, in search of the perfect mate, it is we who attach ourselves to undesirables, to men of little substance, to superficial Sambos, to men with self-destructive impulses who carry us along with them to the brink of pain and disaster. Some of us are in a trance, so obsessed with marriage, so preoccupied with a "real" relationship, that we neglect to be content with what we already have.

We must learn that we don't need a man to prove that we're a woman. Think of the energy and passion we spend chasing men who don't want us. We could spend that time making ourselves happy. It's okay to be single. Not good or bad but simply okay. Truth be told, some of my most creative, productive, and peaceful moments occur when I'm alone, getting in touch with my inner spirit, preparing to march to a different drummer.

The only things we really need to survive in this world—no matter how much we may want—are oxygen, water, and food. We can never predict how someone else is going to treat us, so how can we depend on them for our survival—for our self-respect or self-esteem?

Stop the WIM act. *Woe Is Me! Po' little me!* Women who suffer continuously are boring. If you are always whining and complaining, sooner or later people will start avoiding you. And they should! If you stop feeling sorry for yourself and stop playing the victim, the world might stop treating you like one.

We should not covet our friends' marriages. Everything that glitters is not gold. Many of our married friends are very unhappy. They simply do a good job of hiding it. Many of them wish they were single again. If they were ever divorced, they'd be the first to tell you that they would never get married again.

Just because we can't seem to attract or keep the right man doesn't mean we should wrap ourselves in pity and guilt and fear and pain. Instead, we must spend that energy becoming better sisters and daughters and mothers and aunts. Becoming the best that we can be for ourselves, our family, our friends, and our future.

Not everyone we meet may be in the market for what we have to offer. So we must learn to take some and leave some. Don't overstay your welcome. When the pain starts to outweigh the pleasure, it's time to go. File it under "lesson learned," drop it off at the relationship graveyard, and move on.

We should sit down and have an honest heart-to-heart with ourselves. "I don't seem to be making good choices right now. Maybe I need a relationship break. What can I do to bring more joy and fulfillment into my own life so I don't have to go looking for it in someone else? What can I do to improve the quality of my life so I don't have to depend on someone else to do it for me?"

Stop stepping all over Clark Kent to get to Superman. Learn to ignore the superficial and look for the substance. We'll never find a gold mine looking at the surface.

Behavior, and not words, defines reality. Stop feeding bad behavior by tolerating it. Our behavior tells people how far they can go with us. Put some value on your life. Value yourself for yourself. Stop defining your value by whether or not you have a man. Decide what price you're willing to pay for love. Do you want a relationship at any price? Will you give up your dignity? Your self-respect? Your self-worth? What risks are you willing to take? What rules are you willing to break? Some things should not be negotiable. Our men should take it seriously or take it somewhere else.

We must stop living our lives as a JIC (just in case). "Just in case I find somebody." "Just in case he calls." "Just in case in case." Life is about creating memories. Since tomorrow is not promised to us, we don't have time to wait for someone else to create those memories. We must spend more time thanking God for the life we do have and less time whining about what we don't have.

Being single can be a problem if you perceive it to be a problem. Simply wanting the love, affection, and respect of one man (at a time) is not a bad thing. But if you are preoccupied with having a relationship or obsessed with being married, you might want to do a little soul-searching. If you're emotionally paralyzed anytime you're not involved with someone, you might want to get in touch with your own feelings and your own needs—both emotional and physical. You might want to ask yourself some serious questions.

How do you feel about you? Do you know that love starts at home—with you? Do you see yourself as lovable? If not, why not? If you *need* rather than *want* a man, why? What do you *need* him for? Remember, these are questions that only you can answer. Suppose you never meet "him"? Will you sleepwalk your way through life? Will you settle? What will you settle for? Do you think you could be happy if you never meet that special someone? Are you strong enough to make a conscious decision to be happy without him? Again, these are your questions because this is your life.

In your soul-searching, you may find out that you may be

incapable of loving anyone because you haven't learned to love yourself. You may find out that you need to spend more time getting to know and love yourself and less time looking for someone else to love. You may realize that if you decide to be happy, you can make yourself happy. You can choose to live each day as though it were the last twenty-four hours you have on earth. Who knows? It might be. Life doesn't just happen to us. We make it happen. Every twenty-four hours.

Take a few moments to complete the charts on the following pages. Be honest. It's your book (you paid for it!) and no one has to see it but you. First, a word of caution. Don't start with the obvious in Exercise #1—physical characteristics like tall or short, thin or fat, bald. Don't be concerned about whether or not he has a car or a job. They're important, but right now you should be more concerned about the kind of person he is. Start with qualities like patience, kindness, honesty. Whatever you think is important. Try to be honest with yourself and explain why these qualities are important to you.

In the COMPROMISE column, if your answer is no, explain why. Finally seeing what you want and what you don't want in black and white may give you a rare profile of the person you're looking for. It will also help you determine if your expectations are realistic or completely out in left field. For example, if you want a man who is financially secure (doctor, lawyer, undertaker), it might be a little unrealistic to dream of meeting someone who can stay home every morning and serve you breakfast in bed. Every now and then, maybe, but when is he supposed to earn all that money?

Again, be honest. Nothing is insignificant if it's important to you. If you are a neat, organized person and dream of a neat, organized person to share your uncluttered space, write it down. I don't have to tell you that sometimes it's the little things that make the difference. Just be sure to write yes in the COMPROMISE column if it's something you feel you can give up in order to get something better.

Now, for the hard part. You get a free, unsolicited self-analysis in Exercise #2. You may think you're a saint. Each of us does. But if you're honest, you may have to admit that you're also stubborn, jealous, demanding—you get the picture. It's impossible to do this exercise without looking deep inside your heart and speaking the truth in love. Write that truth down. Make a list of the personality traits you'd like to work on—not necessarily to impress someone else—but because you know you need to. Because you'll be a better person and feel better about yourself.

Don't try to be perfect. We're all human, so it's a little late for that. Just try to be straight with yourself. Be as honest as you can. There are no perfect answers or perfect people (surprise!). In love, there is no norm. So don't worry about your answers. Just be glad that you had the courage to write something down. Study both exercises frequently. Feel free to add, delete, rearrange, or do whatever it takes to make you feel more comfortable with your assessment of who you are and what you want out of this life. If you learn to be your best self and take life exactly the way it's been given to you—abundantly—you won't have to look for happiness. Happiness will come looking for you and chase you down the street.

EXERCISE #1

WHAT I WANT	WHY?	COMPROMISE?
		(If your answer is no, explain)

WHAT I DON'T WANT	WHY?	COMPROMISE?
		(If your answer is no, explain)

EXERCISE #2

A FEW THINGS I LIKE ABOUT ME	A FEW THINGS I'D LIKE TO CHANGE
1.	1.
2.	2.
3.	3.
4.	4.
5.	5.

12

Breaking Up

"Weeping may endure for a night but joy always comes in the morning."

Let's face it. Some of us get lucky and meet men who really do want to make a commitment to love and loving. Unfortunately, even those relationships sometimes end in separation. The end of a relationship can be a devastating experience. But it doesn't have to be.

It's a fact that the world will not end because your relationship does. Expect withdrawal pains, particularly if you cared very deeply for your man. It may be hard but not impossible. The pain will lessen and the wound will eventually heal.

By the way, it's okay to get mad, at least for a while. When you're angry, you'll be less vulnerable and less apt to wallow in self-pity. But be careful not to allow anger to linger too long. When it does, it can become toxic. It makes you sick and the people around you sick. Learn to express your anger, control it, or channel it. And as soon as possible, redirect your energy toward your family and friends, who can be the difference between sanity and going off the deep end. Ultimately, it is you who must love yourself back to good emotional health and get on with your life.

We each have an inner reservoir of strength. When we're hurting, we may have to look deeper to find ours but it's always there, waiting for us to embrace it. Finding it and drawing from it will help you get rid of the ghosts as soon as possible. Too often we give others the power to hurt us, even after they're gone. We must learn to take back some of the power we have given others to hurt us, to disappoint us, to crush our spirits. If you have devoted time getting to know and love yourself, it'll be easier to cope with being alone, even after a traumatic loss.

In the middle of the night, when the pain seems unbearable, don't be afraid to carefully and honestly examine the relationship you're grieving. One thing that will speed your recovery is separating fact from fiction. Ask yourself if what brought the two of you together was strong enough to keep you there. Apparently it wasn't. And since it wasn't, perhaps it was time to say good-bye. Be brutally honest with yourself. You may have known that this was a one-way or dead-end street when you got on it, but you got involved anyway. Don't glamorize it now, after the fact. We have only four options in a relationship: stay and accept it; stay and hate it; change it; or leave. Not everybody you meet is your destiny. If you choose to leave (or he does), accept it for what it was. Good or bad—if it didn't last—it wasn't meant to last.

Some people have different ways of coping with the end of a relationship. (I believe in going cold turkey. If you don't feed it, it'll die. No late-night calls or visits. No "What if we try agains"? If it's over, it's over.) Whatever works for you, do it. The goal is to survive the loss without losing yourself. The goal is to keep your body and spirit from being contaminated with anger and hate and fear. Get on your knees and thank God that Mr. Wrong didn't take your heart and soul with him. Then close the book, dry your tears, and get on with your life.

This may be a great time to remember that you are the main course in your life. Everything else on the menu is gravy. Look at your lost relationship as a stepping-stone, not a stumbling block. This perspective will allow you to be alert so you can recognize the next honest, open, loving man that God may send your way. If you're walking around in a coma or your vision is clouded by tears, you'll probably miss him. If you're walking around unkempt with bad breath and swollen eyes, grieving the loss of something that wasn't meant to be in the first place, your dream man may catch a glimpse of you, shake his head in disbelief, put on his shades, and cross the street.

Losing a lover hurts but it can't kill you. We've all been there. And we've survived. Survival should be your primary motivation. Healing should be your primary goal. Mourning is natural, but it shouldn't last a lifetime. Releasing the pain as soon as possible helps you move from the darkness to the light more quickly. Life always looks better in the light. The light reflects the possibilities that await us on the other side of grief. The light gives us the power to move on to the next chapter in our life. Wipe away the tears, get the lead out of your behind, and thank God you can kiss that hallucination good-bye!

13

Alternatives to Living Single

"Now is the only time you have."

H
ere's the scenario: You're single. You're not involved with anyone special, and you're having difficulty coping with the downtime between boyfriends and lovers. Actually, this is a perfect opportunity to get off the merry-go-round for a minute and enjoy the freedom of being single, to enjoy your space and peace of mind. It's a great chance to renew, recover, regroup, rebound, and reevaluate your life—where you've been and where you're headed.

I know that a lot of people think there's something wrong with you if you even look like you enjoy being single. So it takes a lot of strength and courage to be single and enjoy it, particularly in a society that is preoccupied with love and sex. Love sells records, movies, television, and toilet paper. If you're single and tired of salesmen knocking on your brain telling you that you can't be happy without a mate or if you're tired of perpetually singing the I-want-to-be-in-love wedding-day-anticipation blues, make a commitment to yourself today to start enjoying your life—

with or without a man. Start enjoying your freedom, your opportunities, your choices.

But what—you ask, holding back the tears—could be an alternative to a life of being alone and manless (sounds like a disease, doesn't it?)? If you really cannot envision yourself without a steady man and have no desire to live life without one, here are a few options:

1. **Become a nun.** If you want to deal in absolutes, make a beeline to the nearest convent and don't look back. Only virgins need apply!

2. **Become a ho** (slang for working girl). This is a really sick idea, but if you simply cannot do without a daily dose of sex and prefer men who can't make it with real women, go for it! I can't imagine sleeping with someone who has to pay for a little action, but it's not my decision.

3. **Date White men** (or men from other ethnic groups). Black women have access to a lot of men today but most of us still prefer Black men. If your search for a "good" Black man keeps taking you down one-way streets you may decide to cross over. But think long and think hard. Stepping outside the tribe and crossing over requires a lot of courage. And we still live in America.

4. **Date undesirables** (see chapter 8). Please pray for X-ray vision so you can see the truth about these characters. Most of them are as intelligent as lint and incapable of giving or receiving love. Unless you are prepared to give 200 percent and receive less than 2 percent back, leave these brothers alone! Usually the only thing that they're good at is destruction. The best thing this guy can do *for* you is to *leave* you alone. The best thing *you* can do for *you* is to leave him alone!

5. **Date women.** If you've made a conscious decision to go on a man-diet and experiment with women because you've been hurt

so many times, please don't tell me about it. I'm personally not ready to give up on brothers yet.

6. **Become celibate.** Celibacy is not the worst state you could choose. We don't *need* sex in order to survive. There is nothing in the Constitution or the Bill of Rights that says you must have sex. Having sex is not a requirement of being a good citizen, getting a job, or running a marathon. God has distinguished us from the animals by giving us intellect and will. Unlike the animals, for whom mating is a strictly physical act, human beings generally get to choose if and when and with whom we're going to engage in sexual activity.

Abstaining from sex may be difficult for some people, but it's not impossible. Taking a break from sexual relations and all of the issues we bring with us can be an opportunity to clear your brain and your life. It's a great time to do some self-examination, resist the temptation to conform to the ways of the world, shake bad habits, set new goals, and decide (maybe once and for all) what's really important to you. And for those of us who are trying to walk in the Spirit, celibacy gives us a chance to see sexuality through the eyes of the Creator—as something beautiful to be expressed within the boundaries of marriage.

By the way, celibacy is not new (rumor has it that even the hot-blooded Cleopatra occasionally practiced celibacy). For centuries, people just like you and me have said, "Enough is enough!" They have refused to become physically involved with a member of the opposite sex "just because." I'm always amazed at the reaction of some people when they ask you about your personal life (which is really none of their business) and you tell them that you haven't been with or "known" (in the biblical sense) a man in six months or a year or longer. They seemed surprised and shocked that you could last that long. But some of those same hypocritical people who go into shock with that simple truth will also smile and say, "You go, girl!" if you tell them that you did it with the entire defensive line of the Dallas Cowboys! What's wrong with this picture?

What's wrong with that picture is that the idea that men you care about—and more importantly, desire—magically appear whenever you're sexually excited. They don't! More often than not, they're nowhere to be found. If you prefer undesirables and battle scars that don't heal to celibacy and peace of mind, you might want to save up your pennies and get some professional help.

Celibacy is not a death sentence, but getting involved with an undesirable might be. What does celibacy mean? It means that you will have more time to focus on your spirit woman than your physical woman. Getting in touch with your spiritual self allows you to see the broader picture and where you fit in the universe. Celibacy helps you to put your life in perspective, to get your priorities straight, and to change your focus. By not yielding to the flesh whenever it calls our name, we begin to see ourselves—our wholeness and significance—as separate and apart from whether we have a mate.

Practicing celibacy may mean that you have to take a few more cold showers or spend more time on the treadmill. It may mean that you have to take up a new hobby instead of getting worked up every Friday night watching Michael Douglas and Sharon Stone in *Basic Instinct*. But exercise, cold showers, and new hobbies may be just what the doctor ordered for this season of your life. Don't write off a celibacy break in your quest to find and keep Mr. Right. It may mean the difference between sanity and a straitjacket.

7. **Date a married man.** Becoming the other woman is really the no-alternative alternative. I had to include it in this chapter because as we get older and no closer to getting hitched, some of

us begin to see married men as the solution to being alone. I call this masochistic, self-defeating alternative "bootleg" love. I know you've heard more than just a few of your friends say, "All of the good ones are married!" And even those of us who don't personally agree with this fable will nod our heads and perpetuate the myth to help explain why we're traveling the spring or summer of our life alone.

After all—we say to ourselves—as beautiful and intelligent and successful as we are, what other reasons could there be for our singleness? Surely all of the good ones *are* married! That's bull! And you know it's bull!

Just for the record, not all of the good ones are married. In fact, a lot of the ones who *are* married aren't that good. Not only are they bad for their wives, they'd be worse for you. A married man who "fools" around has already made a definite statement about his character. He's already proven he's a liar, a cheat, and a thief. A thief, you say? Well, he's stealing precious moments from his wife and trying to steal the best years of your life. He's also selfish, dishonest, egotistical, and most of all, untrustworthy, and these are just a few of his defects.

Personally, I have too much love to give to someone who can love me genuinely (and openly) without giving it to a greedy married man. After all, what can he offer you? A few stolen moments in and out of your life maybe twice a week (if you're lucky). No birthdays! No holidays! No week-long vacations for two! No shoulder to cry on late at night after the crazies on your job have made you crazy all day. No warm body to snuggle up to past dawn on a cold and rainy Saturday morning! No one to stay up all night with and watch the sun come up on a beautiful Sunday morning.

What can he offer you? An occasional telephone call, an occasional hot tub, and a lot of heartaches. The question is, Why take the risk? You can get the call, the hot tub, and a lot less heartache with a single man for half the risk. "But there are no single men!" you say, whining. O ye of little faith! I beg to differ. We may not know a lot of single men. And maybe we don't like the ones we do know. But that doesn't mean they aren't out there.

We're out there. And they're out there. Searching . . . just like us. Holding on to their dreams . . . just like us. Waiting to exhale . . . just like us. There may be fewer of them and we may pass like ships in the night, but they are out there. Real men. Men who don't make all their decisions from the waist down. Men who don't go into a coma when you ask for a commitment. Men who don't pretend to be socially retarded when you mention the word *marriage* around them. Real men are out there. I'll never stop believing that. And neither should you.

But that's not the point. Even if we didn't believe there were some good single men out there, it still wouldn't justify dating a married man. Fight the urge to convince yourself that anything is better than nothing, just because you're lonely. And let's not forget that the entire situation becomes even clearer (if you'll take off the rose-colored glasses) when you accept the fact that you're not what he wants either. If he really wanted you, he'd wake up in *your* bed every morning—not his wife's. Think about it.

And think about all of the surveys that point out the extraordinary number of married men who are unfaithful. Why should you become another statistic, particularly when those studies indicate that the majority of these men *do not*, repeat, *do not* divorce their wives to marry the other woman? In fact, there may be numerous other women, since some married men are involved in multiple relationships.

None of us are immune to pain at some point in a relationship. But why allow a selfish, vain, egotistical, lying, worthless, no-good, mangy married jackass to hurt you when a single guy can serve the same purpose without the baggage? In fact, just thinking about a married man who cheats on his wife should make you angry. It's okay. Get angry. Get real angry. How dare he think he can have the best of both worlds—a loving wife and a wifely lover? How dare he think he deserves all the love and tenderness and passion and compassion that you've been saving up all these years? How dare he think you should give him your heart when he can't even give you his phone number? Duh!

The odds are against you from the very beginning. It's a no-win situation with few happy endings. A married man always wants more than he can or will give. His lies will reach epidemic proportions about everything. From why he can't see you on your regular night to whether or not he still sleeps with his wife—although she's three months' pregnant. (Another virgin birth!)

What kind of promises can he make you? How many promises will he have to break because of extenuating circumstances? Becoming the other woman can never be a real alternative for a woman who loves herself and puts a value on her love and her life. Bootleg love can never be an alternative for someone who knows that the price is too high. The question I always ask myself when a married man comes on to me is, Why should *I* share? And the answer is always the same: I shouldn't! And I won't. I'm too selfish to share. Be selfish. It's okay to be a little selfish sometimes. Sometimes, our *self* is all we have!

Nevertheless, if you crave uncertainty in your life, if your IQ is less than your age, and you want a man at any cost, do what you have to do. It's your life. You get to choose. But just between the two of us, you should never want to become *a* woman in your man's life but *the* woman in his life.

14

Choosing Love Now

"You wouldn't have to count the days if you made each day count!"

If you've resigned yourself to leading a meaningless, unhappy, unfulfilled life just because you're single, you deserve a meaningless, unhappy, unfulfilled life. But if you have accepted the fact that you may not ever get married and that either way you're going to be okay, then you're already on your way to a life worth living and loving. The fact is that not every available single woman is going to get married. Some of us may never be blessed with an exclusive, long-term relationship, and even if some of us are blessed with and end up in what we believe is an ideal relationship, it may not lead to matrimony.

But none of these facts give us license to magnify the problem, ignore our options, and dwell in a continuous state of depression because of the void in our lives. Frankly, it was because of this void in my own life that I was inspired by God to write this book. I'm here to tell you that you don't have to feel powerless anymore. You have the power and the authority to change your life. You don't have to waste precious time and energy getting stuck in Why? "Why me?" Why not you? "Life isn't fair!" Who said it would be?

Today's single Black woman is just another test of Black womanhood—of our strength and endurance. She is a testimony to countless other Black women whose problems far surpassed that of living alone. Real problems, like how to stay on your feet in a cotton field when it's ninety degrees and you're eight months' pregnant. How to keep your baby from being sold the moment he leaves the comfort of your womb. How to make your man feel like a man for a few hours every night when he's been on his knees all day. How to stay alive.

If there is a single thread that holds all Black people together, it is endurance dipped in faith and polished with hope. Black women wrote the book on endurance. We are the original victors, but we've had our share of experiences as victims.

We've been victims of the racism of slavery and the bigotry of Jim Crow that stripped our men of their self-respect and pride.

We've been victims of the Vietnam War and the violence and turmoil of the '60s that robbed us of Black men of character, strength, courage, and vision.

We've been victims of the crack epidemic that threatens to destroy another generation of young Black men and boys—our fathers and uncles and brothers and sons.

We're at risk of being victims of poverty, pimps, prostitution, alcoholism, drug addiction, STDs (including AIDS), child abuse, domestic violence, and pseudosophisticated three-piece-suit-wearing professional Uncle Toms from corporate boardrooms to the Supreme Court. And let's not forget all those Mr. Charlies who refuse to share the power.

Unfortunately, we have also been victims of our own men, who—because they control so little in America—try to control us with fear and insecurity, pride and pain. Trust me! Black chauvinism is alive and living in this sexist, racist society that we love so much.

We're living proof that there are victims. But we cannot afford the luxury of acting like victims. We can't even afford to identify with the victim. Why? Black women have never been totally dependent on our men for everything. From African deserts to Southern plantations to inner-city tenements, we've always carried our share of the load, often more than our share. Although Black men and women are still getting married, having children, and building lives together, a disproportionate number of single Black women are still carrying the load: for Black children, for the Black family, for the Black community. So waiting for Mr. Right to ride into our lives and rescue us is just not consistent with reality.

The reality is that putting all of our energies into finding that "perfect" mate is robbing us of some of the best years of our lives. Our consuming desire to find Mr. Right hangs over most of us like a shadow. We're holding out for that mystical, magical, long-term permanent relationship.

Everything in our lives is temporary. Rather than buy a home, we choose to live in a 300-square-foot sardine can of an apartment because we tell ourselves that "buying a house is so permanent. It's something my husband and I will invest in one day." Well, if you ever meet Mr. Right, you can buy a bigger house together.

You refuse to take vacations because "everybody says that single women shouldn't travel alone! What happens if I meet somebody special and he wants to go somewhere I've already been?" Duh! First of all, who is everybody and why should you care what they think? Where would you go? How about the rest of the world, girlfriend?

And don't forget about buying that beautiful diamond ring that you've been admiring for the past five years! You'd really like to buy it for your birthday, but everybody knows that "women shouldn't buy themselves diamonds"! Why not? If you ever meet Mr. Right, he can buy you another one!

"But what about babies?" What about them? You want children? Have a little talk with God and the two of you decide. You don't have to ask your mother, your friend, or your neighbor. As long as you don't have them by a married man and can afford to take care of them yourself, have them. Adopt them. It's your decision . . . and your life. Do your homework, though. Raising a child by yourself is not a piece of cake. It can be tough, very tough. Yet in spite of that, single women are choosing to have children every day. Frankly, I'd rather see a child brought into this world by a bright, intelligent, self-sufficient, single Black woman than by a lot of other people who are dropping babies all over the place every nine months.

"But what will people think?" Two words: Forget people! Unless they're paying your house note, car note, grocery bill, utility bill, and MasterCard in full each month, forget 'em! Your creator is the only one you have to answer to. And between you and me, I think God is too busy trying to save humanity to be overly concerned about a self-supporting single woman who wants to love and nurture another human being. But don't take my word for it. Pray about it!

I could go on and on with the list of what people think single women can't and shouldn't do just because they're single. You and I both know that all of it is bull! But we're so busy letting other people project their expectations on us because we're single that we fall into the trap anyway. After thirty-five or forty or fifty years of socialization, many of us will look back on our lives and wonder how we allowed ourselves to have so many unlived experiences—like buying a house, taking a cruise, or going to the Holy Land.

But even beyond those unlived experiences, it is the unfulfilled human potential that is most damaging. We are so busy preparing for a future with someone else that we never fully develop the person who has always been our best friend and companion—ourselves. We owe it to ourselves (and to the men who may come into our lives) to develop ourselves and our potential to the fullest. We shouldn't use the possibility of never finding that special relationship as an excuse to put our personal growth on hold. Most relationships have a better chance of surviving if two whole people come together, not two halves.

We are our greatest personal asset but we will never be able to see the beauty of our own world if we refuse to accept and take responsibility for our own happiness. I simply will not explain or apologize for being single. When people ask me why I'm single, I always give the same answer: Because I haven't met the man that makes my life better than it is already! No, my life isn't perfect. Yes, I've got my share of ups and downs. Who hasn't? But overall, it's pretty damn good considering the alternatives (see chapter 13). I rest my case.

If your life isn't so good right now, maybe it's time that you asked yourself why. Have you accepted responsibility for your own happiness? If not, why not? Are you still holding your breath, waiting for someone to tell you how special you are? *You* can do that! Are you still angry, mourning the loss of someone who's come and gone, someone who wasn't even that great when you stop to think about it? Are you being consumed by feelings of despair or loneliness instead of directing your energies to positive things and people who build you up rather than tear you down? Are you still waiting for your ship to come in rather than launching it yourself? It's never too late to develop new interests and hobbies, learn new skills, meet new friends, and make new discoveries about yourself and life.

Black women have shown throughout our history in this country that we have unlimited potential—despite three hundred years of racist, sexist attitudes. As someone once said, "We have done so much with so little for so long that we think we can do anything in no time flat!" Today, we have unlimited opportunities and choices to complement our potential. For years, we have been content to settle for less—less money for our labor, less credit for our contributions, less commitment from our men. In short, we have not only had to fight off the chains of racism but the shackles of second-class citizenship because—through no fault of our own—we were born women.

It's almost the twenty-first century and many of us are still in the twilight zone—somewhere between here and now and there and nowhere. We simply can't afford to sleepwalk through our lives just because we're single women. We cannot continue to impersonate human beings, waiting for some unreliable prop who may or may not be right for us to breathe life into our lifeless bodies and spirits. We and we alone are responsible for our happiness and our peace of mind.

And being happy or at peace doesn't mean assuming a defeatist attitude, giving up ever finding that man you think may be perfect for you, who may bring you joy and happiness. Your name could be on a blessing that's headed your way right now. Your Mr. Right could be out there . . . somewhere . . . looking . . . waiting for you. But he may be walking. He may be lost, so in the meantime . . . be happy! Be content with where you are . . . now . . . in your life. And know that, with or without a mate, you will survive.

How—not if—you survive becomes the million-dollar question. Since it is your life, it becomes your question. You can choose to sit idly by and watch your twenties, thirties, and forties slip by. Or you can take charge of your life this very moment and make it an unforgettable experience, an extraordinary happening, today and everyday. And even if you never find exactly who or what you're looking for, you may find something greater by living each day to the fullest. Greater rewards. Greater contentment. Greater happiness.

If you want to change your life, start with your attitude. Just rearranging things on the outside won't help unless you're ready to do work on the inside. We have to update our attitude about men, about sex, about being alone. No man can make you feel good about yourself if *you* don't feel good about yourself. How's your confidence? Your self-esteem? Do you have a sense of humor? Learning to laugh at the mysteries of life will give you a brand-new perspective on life.

Somehow we have given ourselves permission to act like victims and we've become crippled in the process. We're confused. And if we have a problem seeing the issue clearly and objectively, how do we expect our men to understand our feelings, our frustrations, our fears? What's the real issue? It's not whether or not being married or single is right or wrong. The issue is not whether we—as single Black women—want to be single. Many of us don't. The real issue is whether we can adjust to being single for the rest of our life if we have to. The issue is whether we can create a meaningful life and meaningful relationships with people who may not be around for the duration. The issue is whether we are willing to live in the present or wait for the future to catch up with us.

I think we can do anything we choose to. We can turn this so-called shortage of good men into an opportunity to learn to love ourselves. To develop our God-given talents. To appreciate the things that we sometimes take for granted—good health, good friends, loving parents, a decent job, a nice house, a car that runs, you name it. Being single gives us an opportunity to learn and grow and be anything we want to be, accepting life the way it is but knowing that change is inevitable and that this too shall pass.

We can learn to say "thank you" for the qualities that make life worth living. Love. Joy. Peace. We can learn to complete the circle of love on our own. We can learn to love ourselves so much that, with or without a man in our lives, we still know that we are loved.

There is no doubt in my mind that I am loved! God loves me! My family loves me! My friends love me! And most importantly, I love me! I'm alive! I'm healthy! And my life is unfolding just the way it should. Believe it or not, your life is unfolding just the way it should. You're alive and somebody, somewhere loves you (God and you are a majority).

Start counting the blessings that flow in and out of your life every day. Then count the minutes, hours, days, weeks, months, and years you've spent worrying, whining, and complaining about that one missing slice from the pie of life—a man—when the rest of the pie has been yours for the taking. Choose love now, with or without a mate, and live each precious moment of your life loving you!

"We will either find a way or make one!"